OTHER VOLUMES IN THIS SERIES

THE

BEST

AMERICAN

POETRY

2000

◊ ◊ ◊

Rita Dove, Editor

David Lehman, Series Editor

SCRIBNER

NEW YORK LONDON TORONTO SYDNEY SINGAPORE

SCRIBNER
1230 Avenue of the Americas
New York, NY 10020

Set in Bembo

Manufactured in the United States of America

1   3   5   7   9   10   8   6   4   2

ISBN 0-684-84281-5
ISSN 1040-5763

CONTENTS

David Lehman was born in New York City in 1948. Educated at Columbia and Cambridge universities, he earned his doctorate in English, taught at Hamilton College, then left academe to take his chances as a freelance writer. He is the author of four poetry books, most recently *The Daily Mirror: A Journal in Poetry* (Scribner, 2000). His nonfiction books include *The Last Avant-Garde: The Making of the New York School of Poets* (Doubleday, 1998) and *The Perfect Murder,* his study of detective novels, which appeared in a revised paperback edition in 2000 (Michigan). With Star Black he is codirector of the KGB Bar poetry reading series in New York City and coeditor of *The KGB Bar Book of Poems* (Harper-Collins, 2000). He has served on the core faculty of the graduate writing programs at Bennington College and the New School since the inception of both programs, in 1994 and 1996 respectively. He also teaches "Great Poems" as an honors course for undergraduates at NYU. A Guggenheim Fellow, he succeeded Donald Hall as general editor of the University of Michigan Press's Poets on Poetry series. He initiated *The Best American Poetry* in 1988.

FOREWORD

by David Lehman

◊   ◊   ◊

At the Poetry International Festival in Rotterdam in June 1999, a symposium of poets, critics, and editors convened to discuss the state of the art in our various nations. Orhan Koçak of Turkey summed up one familiar complaint: "hypertrophy of supply, atrophy of demand." Several delegates mentioned the decline of good, disinterested, practical criticism. "The best critics are the poets themselves," Poland's Adriana Szymanska said, but Jonas Ellerström, the Swedish publisher, countered that most poet-critics preach to the converted, and the group debated whether critics should or should not be poets themselves. Have poetry readings made as great an impact elsewhere as in North America? Yes, as became clear when Gus Ferguson (South Africa), coining a sort of retroactive neologism along the lines of "snail mail," spoke of "page poetry" to distinguish it from the recited kind. Ferguson warned about the "therapy culture" invading poetry. Al Creighton (Guyana) sounded a more enthusiastic note, dwelling on performance poetry, the influence of reggae music, the use of Creole rhythms and speech, and the "integration of the popular and the literary" in Caribbean verse. Most of the participants agreed that public interest in poetry has grown considerably over the last decade. Christoph Buchwald (Germany) pointed to the popularity of poetry anthologies, Alex Susanna (Spain) to the success of poetry festivals, Marc Reugebrink (Holland) to civic-minded initiatives that put lines of verse on buildings and trucks, Joachim Sartorius (Germany) to poets whose rapport with audiences disproves the charge that poetry is hopelessly elitist and exclusionary.

After three such three-hour sessions, the group crystallized an issue full of paradox that agitated all. The United States was not alone in witnessing a resurgence of poetry. Yet so many manifestations of the poetry boom deserved no laurels on their merits. What did we make of the extraordinary flowering of bad poetry so evident in so many places? In short, is bad poetry bad or good for poetry? Does it devalue the art, lower expectations, diminish the public's capacity to embrace the real thing when it comes along? Or is it a sign that poetry is thriving though not necessarily in ways calculated to win the approval of academies? Michael Schmidt, the poet who heads Britain's Carcanet Press, declared unequivocally that bad poetry is bad for poetry, because it cannot but "coarsen taste and sensibility." Jack Shoemaker, the respected publisher of Counterpoint Press in Washington, D.C., quoted Ezra Pound's dictum that every bad poem you read requires a remedy of six good ones to undo the damage. As Jack's American colleague at the conference, I found it easy to understand and sympathize with this point of view. Who would defend sloppy, sentimental, foolish, demagogic, hackneyed, or self-ingratiating verse? We who love poetry dislike it when it fails to meet our expectations. Inevitably, most poems will disappoint readers spoiled by "To His Coy Mistress," "Tintern Abbey," or "Crossing Brooklyn Ferry."

The series editor of *The Best American Poetry* can hardly wish to speak up for mediocre verse or worse. Still, I can't help thinking that the rapid proliferation of poems in unexpected quarters (bus and subway placards, highway billboards, TV sitcoms and commercials) and unusual forms (competitive slams) from unconventional bards (rock-and-roll troubadors, rap artists) argues for the vitality of poetry today. Doesn't poetry belong as much in bars and breweries as in classrooms and libraries? And if the bad poems declaimed at such venues outnumber the good, is that not true of all venues? Rather than feel threatened, mightn't we borrow or steal what is useful and new and adapt it as we will, discarding what we judge to be meretricious?

The hip-hop performance poems of the slam (dunk) generation have influenced not only rap singers but mainstream poets. At a reading at the KGB Bar in New York's East Village in November 1999, Craig Arnold demonstrated a surprising continuity between the formal requirements of traditional well-wrought verse and the slam poet's performance techniques. Arnold read "Hot," a rigorously formal poem, in couplets, from the 1998 edition of this anthology. He had memorized the poem, as an actor would memorize a soliloquy, and he performed it gesturally, as if the bar were an impromptu theater. It was exhilarating, a different pleasure, not necessarily superior to the pleasure of reading the poem on the page but a pleasure assuredly all the same.

Of course, there are distinctions to be made. We constantly (and by "we" I mean not only the editors of *The Best American Poetry* but readers everywhere) sort out the good from the bad, the best from the better, though this is quite a complicated process as our opinions change all the time. We also separate poems from other forms of writing that look like poems. Both poems and song lyrics are in verse, but poems are written to be read and songs are written to be sung or played, and there is little to be gained in obscuring this fundamental difference. I admire the lyrics of, say, Johnny Mercer or Lorenz Hart as much as anyone but feel no need to claim them for the dominion of poetry.* At the same time, I don't complain when *Rolling Stone* examines rock-and-roll lyrics as one would examine poems, for to do so implicitly pays a compliment to poetry as the criterion art, the art by which others ask to be tested. I am less happy with the stubborn notion that poetry is pitiable, a "money-losing proposition," a "perennial stepchild of publishing," and I dislike the sneer of condescension with which the purist treats any poet or poetry impresario who becomes popular or successfully popularizers others. Sometimes I suspect that the critic who deplores the *best* in the title of this series on the grounds that it is putatively elitist secretly resents the fact that the books are popular, have an audience, and have successfully brought poetry to the people instead of keeping it locked up in a museum case.

Poetry's invasion of space formerly verse-free continues apace. When the star of MTV's *Daria* signs up to read for residents of the Better Days Retirement House, she chooses Allen Ginsberg's "Howl," which is a little like reading aloud the opening of Camus's *The Stranger* to one's mother in a hospital bed ("Mother died today," that book begins). Ginsberg's famous battle cry for the Beats echoed in the mind of novelist Gary Krist, who contributed an op-ed column to the *New York Times* on the best minds of his generation, "who hollow-eyed and caffeine-charged sat up surfing the number-choked screens, whispering the bone-cold litany of Amazon, Cisco, AOL." Who says business and poetry are incompatible? Not Wallace Stevens, who opined that "Money is a form of poetry," demurring however from suggesting that the inverse was true. John Barr, the head of an investment banking firm specializing in public utilities, published *Grace,* an epic poem in loose hexameters, with Story Line Press in 1999. In "Street Life," Andrew Serwer's daily on-line column, the *Fortune* magazine writer reported that the CEO and founder of e-academy.com had written a poem entitled "Metaphysics, Microsoft, and Me" in the waiting room outside Bill Gates's office. The anagrams of "AOL Time Warner Inc," which an unidentified Serwer cor-

---

*Nothing resembling consensus exists on this point. Eleanor Wilner chooses Hart's lyric for the immortal Rodgers and Hart standard "The Lady Is a Tramp" as her "poetic first-love," while hard-nosed critic Christopher Ricks conducts seminars on Bob Dylan, bringing Keats, Hopkins, and Eliot to bear on the subject.

respondent contributed after the merger of the two firms, had an avant-garde edge: "I'm a clarinet owner. / Now air-mail center. / Rectilinear woman. / New alarm in erotic. / Win oriental cream."

Margaret Edson's *Wit,* which makes generous use of John Donne's "Holy Sonnets," won the 1999 Pulitzer Prize in drama. The play, about a Donne scholar's losing battle with cancer, makes metaphysical analogies and cunning conceits. "Now I know how poems feel," says the play's heroine regarding her initial days in the hospital, when she is tested, analyzed, critiqued. Eight chemotherapy sessions are like eight "strophes." The protagonist of David Hirson's *Wrong Mountain,* which deserved a better fate than its mixed reviews and short run on Broadway, is a poet consumed from within by the worms of bitterness, resentment, and envy. He suffers from a condition that many of his real-life counterparts know all too well; he has gone, as John Lahr wrote in *The New Yorker,* "from inspiration to publication without circulation." The poets Hirson quotes include W. H. Auden and John Ashbery. Auden's poetry also figures in Tom Bogdan's dance piece, *Tell Me the Truth about Love,* while Tom Stoppard's new play, *The Invention of Love,* focuses on the life, love, and verse of A. E. Housman.

In this presidential election year, David McCullough, Harry Truman's biographer, told columnist Maureen Dowd that the electorate would do well to quiz candidates for the Oval Office on their favorite poem and on the best speech they have ever heard. In January, when Bill Parcells retired as head coach of the New York Jets, he recited a somewhat obscure poem entitled "The Guy in the Glass" by Dale Wimbrow (1934): "You may fool the whole world down the pathway of life / And get pats on the back as you pass, / But your final reward will be heartaches and tears / If you've cheated the man in the glass." The *New York Post* printed the poem in full. During the terrific Super Bowl game between the Rams and Titans on the last Sunday in that month, a stylish black-and-white commercial for Monster.com, the on-line employment service, showed a variety of people and children reciting the opening and closing lines of Robert Frost's "The Road Not Taken." A few months later, a TV commercial for AIG, the insurance behemoth, quoted a meaty chunk of "The Love Song of J. Alfred Prufrock" to warn against the pitfalls of risk-averse behavior.

Poetry has become newsworthy. When Random House and the University of Pittsburgh Press fought over the rights to Billy Collins's poems, the *New York Times* covered the controversy on its front page (below the fold). When two publishers vie for a poet's work, I suppose it does merit front-page treatment. On the other hand, a spate of life-style articles demonstrated either that "all bad poetry springs from genuine feeling" (Oscar Wilde) or that value judgments are sometimes beside the point. On the same day in February 2000 the *Times* printed verse from a twice-monthly retirees' writing workshop in Galveston, Texas, while *U.S.A. Today* broke the story of the three Seattle poets ("a grad student, a new mother, and a modern dancer who works as a barista, or espresso bartender") who collaborate on spontaneous poems as a novelty act at coffee bars. The *New Republic* weighed in that week with the story of a high school basketball legend whose life went to pieces. The article concludes with the player's rap poem ("Father, you put me here / Please show me some sign / Shed some light on this life, especially mine / Confused and scared since the age of nine / You got that white chalk now draw me a white line"). Certainly an element of self-parody enters into some of the promotional activities involving poetry and its uses as therapy, entertainment, and self-expression. The British proved they could be as silly as we when Andrew Motion, who succeeded Ted Hughes as England's poet laureate, agreed to write a poem for a Herefordshire lavatory wall. The project has a name: "Poems on the Throne." Motion said he hoped people would resist "the urge to make puns on my name." At the Poetry Olympics held at the Brooklyn Brewery in November 1999, the NYU team received extra points for saying "who cares" when asked to identify Britain's current poet laureate.

Speaking of indignities, poor Robert Lowell. I have long felt that the corrections column in a newspaper is an underrated pleasure. The June 1999 issue of *Harper's* called attention to a classic of the genre, which, with the logic of a pun, had to do with the documented popularity of poetry writing at correctional facilities. Editor Ron Offen of the always lively magazine *Free Lunch* announced his "sad duty to report that a poem in our special section of prisoner poetry in our last issue" had been plagiarized from a section of Robert Lowell's "My Last Afternoon with Uncle Devereux Winslow" in *Life Studies*. The kicker: "To add insult to injury, I asked the plagiarist for revisions of Lowell's lines on two separate occasions."*

---

*The editor of *Free Lunch* has plenty of company. It is has come to our attention that Jacqueline Dash's poem, "Me Again," chosen for *Best American Poetry 1996* from *In Time*, a journal of poems from a women's prison, was apparently copied almost verbatim from Pablo Neruda's "Me Again," admirably translated by Ben Belitt, in Neruda's *Five Decades, 1925–1970* (Grove Press, 1974). We regret the error and enthusiastically direct our readers to the true source.

The Best American Poetry may disturb the universe of purists or pessimists, for it is testament to the belief that good poetry may be distinguished from bad or merely "competent" verse—and that poetry of intelligence and ambition, sophistication and passion, wit and pathos, can be published to the profit of all. Each year a different guest editor, herself or himself a distinguished poet, makes the selections, thus ensuring that there will be a certain amount of desirable discontinuity from year to year. Rita Dove, the guest editor of this volume, was a natural choice. Born in Akron, Ohio, in 1952, the daughter of a research chemist, she came to the fore in 1987, the year she won the Pulitzer Prize for her book *Thomas and Beulah.* At the time, she was only the second African-American poet to be thus honored. Beginning in 1993 she served for two years as U.S. poet laureate, preceding Robert Hass and Robert Pinsky at that post. All three have been activists, determined to raise the national consciousness of poetry, and it was Rita Dove who virtually redefined the office to this end. She has written verse drama (*The Darker Face of the Earth,* an adaptation of *Oedipus Rex* set on a cotton plantation in the South) that has been performed in the United States as well as in England. Her own poems set store by their clarity; she refuses to make a fetish of difficulty. And at the same time that Dove has committed herself to bring poetry to the people, she has also, in assembling this anthology, invoked high standards of excellence in evaluating the many hundreds of poems that begged for our attention. More than forty magazines yielded poems for this volume; more than twice as many were considered and admired.

The greatest diversity consistent with the highest quality remains the goal of this series. In *The Best American Poetry 2000* we have rhymed verse as well as prose poems, poems consisting of both prose and verse, a villanelle, a double sestina, a truncated pantoum, poems that do the work of apology, elegy, salutation, and homage, narrative poems, a variation on an abecedarium. The first poem in the book (arranged, as always, in alphabetical order) begins with a tragic scene, a rape and murder; the last poem ends with the daffodils shooting out of the earth in spring and the snow covering all in winter. Between the two, the poets address subjects ranging from jazz to botany, the American family in the eyes of an au pair girl from France, the English literary canon, Mary Todd Lincoln, Henry Clay, the painter Pissarro, postfeminism, semiotics, semantics, fathers and mothers, the Vietnam War, love, work, and death. We mark the arrival of the new millennium with a special feature, "The Best American Poetry of the Twentieth Century," for which the current and previous guest editors of this series were asked to nominate their favorite American poems.

Against expectation ours has turned out to be a period favorable to the poetic imagination. The proliferation of webzines and Web sites receptive to poetry suggests the compatibility of the ancient art of verse with leading-edge technology. (According to Lycos, poetry was that search engine's eighth most popular "search term" in 1999, behind Pokémon and *Star Wars* but ahead of tattoos, golf, Jennifer Lopez, pregnancy, guns, and Las Vegas.) Poems can be posted for the public to read within hours of their composition, and the knowledge of this possibility may spur the writer to write more poems, or different ones. Like poetry readings and slams, then, the internet can be construed as a threat to "page poetry." Yet I would not so quickly write off the pleasures of the tangible book, hardcover or paperbound, which you can take with you anywhere, which you can annotate as you peruse, and which shall in time occupy its destined place on the shelf where you keep a record of your history as a reader.

Rita Dove was born in Akron, Ohio, in 1952. A 1970 Presidential Scholar, she received her B.A. summa cum laude from Miami University of Ohio and her M.F.A. from the University of Iowa. She held a Fulbright scholarship at Universität Tübingen in Germany. Her poetry collections include *The Yellow House on the Corner* (1980), *Museum* (1983), *Thomas and Beulah* (1986), *Grace Notes* (1989), *Selected Poems* (1993), *Mother Love* (1995), and *On the Bus with Rosa Parks* (Norton, 1999). In 1987 she received the Pulitzer Prize in poetry. She is also the author of a book of short stories, *Fifth Sunday* (1985), a novel, *Through the Ivory Gate* (1992), a volume of essays, *The Poet's World* (1995), and a play, *The Darker Face of the Earth*, which had its world premiere in 1996 at the Oregon Shakespeare Festival and was subsequently produced at the Kennedy Center in Washington, D.C., and, in August 1999, at the Royal National Theatre in London. *Seven for Luck*, a song cycle for soprano and orchestra with music by John Williams, was premiered by the Boston Symphony at Tanglewood in the summer of 1998. She served as Poet Laureate of the United States and Consultant in Poetry to the Library of Congress from 1993 to 1995 and was reappointed Special Consultant in Poetry in 1999. She is Commonwealth Professor of English at the University of Virginia in Charlottesville, where she lives with her husband, the German writer Fred Viebahn, and their daughter, Aviva.

INTRODUCTION

by Rita Dove

◊   ◊   ◊

Fame is a vapor, popularity is accident; the only earthly certainty is oblivion.

—MARK TWAIN

Poised on the lip of a century—even if such brimming is just a metaphor—America puffs up its chest, medals jiggling. We still imagine ourselves the leaders of the Free World; but what are we leading? A mere decade ago we were so sure of ourselves, standing in front of the iron curtain, whence all the smoke and bellowing emerged; then Toto pulled the drapes aside and we gawked, disappointed: Was that all there was? If the enemy turns out to be a doddering old man who has lost his way home, what does that make us, who so earnestly fought him?

Of course the poets knew this long ago. Or did we? "The unacknowledged legislators of the world," Shelley called us. After World War II, the Beats hammered at the formicaed complacency of the new suburbia; the best minds of Ginsberg's acquaintance joined forces with the Black Arts movement to lead the insurgence into the sixties, when women asserted their right to write the body feminine and to redeem the body politic. Buffeted by social forces, poets male and female dove into the wreck, only to discover a thousand and one ways both to be in the world and to report on it: by exposing one's own steaming liver (confessionalists), by making the intolerable bearable through elegance of presentation (formalism), by beguiling the reader to take in the world through the refracting lens of the poet's personality (New York School), or by refracting the very medium of communication (language poets). With Robert Frost's famed tennis net long down, poets struck off in different directions, trying to restring that net or to defy it: Deep Image. Composition by Field. Flat Style. Call and Response. Prose Poem. New Formalism. Lyric Narrative. Dramatic Monologue. Slam Poetry.

But is any of this so very new? After all, this is a country that produced two very different blossoms early on—Walt Whitman and Emily Dickinson—from the same fertile soil. Even that master of caged music and admirer of the "still unravish'd bride of quietness," John Keats, admitted, "There is nothing stable in the world; uproar's your only music."

Apologia

The questions which one asks oneself begin, at last, to illuminate the world, and become one's key to the experience of others.
                                                    —JAMES BALDWIN

Whenever I am called upon to introduce a poetry reading, I quake. It's a tricky role to play, an often thankless and (hopefully) selfless task, for it falls upon the introducer to prepare the audience for the evening—to serve as an airlock between the roaring bluster of the world's obligations and the still center of being that good poetry awakens. To serve this transition, a good introduction must reach beyond the facts to become more than just a mere recital of the poet's credentials and biographical dates—which in many ways is but a pale reminder of the quantified world outside. Without upstaging the poet, the introducer should ease us into his other worldview, evoking a mood that the waiting poet will step into as into a spotlight configured with the precise gels to complement her complexion and build. For the introduction's space of time, the audience should cling to every word, much as the Egyptologist raptly follows hieroglyphics in order to gain entry to a secret chamber; once entry is attained, however, the entryway is left behind, its memory flushed away in the rapture of discovery.

But the word "introduce"—which actually means "to lead in(ward)," from the Latin *introducere: intro,* or within, and *ducere,* to lead—entails more than merely pointing the way and opening the door. The word (and the gesture) shares a root with a host of treacherous relatives: *conduce, induce, produce, reduce, seduce, subdue, traduce,* even that cocky know-it-all *deduce* (and its shadowy cousin, *deduct*): It is a beguiler, this root, shifting shape to fit the hat it dons. In our case here, it should be a companion who takes you inside the gates. What happens next is up to you—you may look back for advice or you may opt to be guided solely by your own impressions, glad to be rid of such well-meaning associations.

So: I am your untrustworthy guide. I can promise wonders inside, but you must find them on your own. A confrontation with poetry should provoke a journey into yourself: You may argue with my choices, argue with the poems themselves, perhaps even argue with the year they represent; but I hope boredom will not be an option.

In choosing these seventy-five poems, arranged alphabetically according to author, I have eschewed the illusions of theme and formal classification: Pure lyrics float before rangy narratives, the political bristles beside the elegiac. You may notice a proliferation of gardens and flowers, particularly roses (Elton Glaser's "And in the Afternoons I Botanized," Frank X. Gaspar's "Seven Roses," Stanley Plumly's "Kunitz Tending Roses," and Susan Wood's "Analysis of the Rose as Sentimental Despair") and stop your browsing to muse briefly on paradise lost; but I hope you would also be reminded of Rilke's poem "A Bowl of Roses," where contemplation of the arranged blooms prompts a warning not to make too absolute a symbol of any object. "What can't they be?" he asks us:

> And aren't all that way: simply self-containing,
> if self-containing means: to transform the world outside
> and the wind and the rain and the patience of spring
> and guilt and restlessness and muffled fate
> and even the changing and flying and fleeing of the clouds
> and the vague influence of the distant stars
> into a handful of inwardness.
>
> (Trans. Edward Snow)

I will not claim Objectivity in my selections. Subjectivity is what makes life interesting and turns human history into a kaleidoscope of wills meeting accidents. I am proud to recognize established masters of the art such as Mary Oliver, Donald Justice, Richard Wilbur, and Lucille Clifton, but I am just as thrilled by authors previously unknown to me: Denise Duhamel, Linh Dinh, Christopher Edgar, Marsha Janson.

My method was simple: Read the poems without looking at the author's name, if possible, and put aside for further consideration only those pieces which made me catch my breath. The final criterion was Emily Dickinson's famed description—if I felt that the top of my head had been taken off, the poem was in. Sometimes a poem failed the scalping test on first reading; but if any passage caused a prickling of the skin, I would put it aside and return to it on another day, in another mood, for I was always wary of the power of mood and energy level on one's receptivity to any serious work—and every poem, no matter how seemingly effortless or joyous, should be serious work.

Yet there are factors in each of our lives that figure into our perception of the world around us, the reality we embody. As readers we bring our own emotional baggage to the page, where it will accompany us on the journey, perhaps weighing us down, perhaps coming in handy if we recognize the particular weather in the world of the text. I can only guess at my own biases, but I can admit to you some of the preoccupations that may have colored my decisions. Two autumns ago, lightning struck my house and the resulting fire destroyed most of it. Significant portions of my and my husband's literary archive, personal correspondence, notebooks, and early drafts were consumed by the inferno. My husband's study was Ground Zero, and my study was drenched by the firemen's hoses, so that notebooks with inked entries were rendered unreadable. Most of our library either burned or suffered mildew; clothes, memorabilia, furniture, etc.—gone.

After such efficient devastation, I found it difficult to tolerate frivolity or indulgence—particularly in poetry. Humor was a saving virtue, but gratuitous anecdotes grated on my literary nerves. Has my personal experience, therefore, resulted in a preponderance of gloomy poems? I don't believe so. Extremes of grief and violence are certainly present, but so, too, in ample measure are celebration and laughter.

As a consequence of the fire and the consistent frustrations of rebuilding, my husband and I decided to dash it all and dance on the ashes . . . literally. We took up ballroom dancing, and the pleasures and rigors of this sport have meshed quite neatly with my long-held convictions about my vocation: that a poem must sing, even if the song elicits horror. That no poem is ever completely free of the rules, whether those rules are formally imposed from the outset or arise as the poem takes shape, informed by the language and objects that constitute its matrix. That emotion is never an excuse for verbosity, but a poem without feeling is like a gaudy piece of costume jewelry that will shatter under the least pressure.

There is also the bias of Time: this blasted millennium mania, which seemed to infuse every aspect of daily life (down to Millennium M&Ms), may have trickled into *The Best American Poetry 2000* as well. Shouldn't this volume speak of our dreams and failures, desires and fears? I have tried to resist the pull of Pronouncement and Prophecy while remembering both Wittgenstein's call to commitment ("The world is everything that is the case") and Dylan Thomas, who said of poetry: "I like to think of it as statements made on the way to the grave."

Yet while navigating the mountains of magazines that amassed in my study over the past year, I could not help but notice certain trends, like reading the route of the landscape of our time: a yearning to break down the barrier of small talk by fracturing the language (Brenda Hillman's "Air for Mercury," Olena Kalytiak Davis's "Six Apologies, Lord," John Yau's haunting "Borrowed Love Poems"), as well as the deliberate fracturing of small talk by embracing it (Denise Duhamel's exploded sestina "Incest Taboo"; the colloquial ferocity of Barbara Hamby's "Ode to the Lost Luggage Warehouse at the Rome Airport"; Paul Violi's shaggy dog story "As I Was Telling David and Alexandra Kelley"). There is the trajectory of History in Julianna Baggott's "Mary Todd on Her Deathbed" and the coy counterpoint of grand thoughts and anecdote in Thomas Lux's wryly wrought "Henry Clay's Mouth." There is also the interpolation of personal chronicles with the larger sweep of events (Jean Nordhaus's "Aunt Lily and Frederick the Great," Donald Platt's "History & Bikinis"). Some poets rage against humanity for its complacency in the face of prejudice and cruelty (Yusef Komunyakaa's "The Goddess of Quotas Laments," Rebecca Seiferle's "Welcome to Ithaca," Reginald Shepherd's "Semantics at Four P.M."), while others lament our helplessness (Richard Siken's "The Dislocated Room," Jim Daniels's "Between Periods"). Still others write with devastating irony (Adrienne Su's "The English Canon," Carolyn Kizer's "The Oration") or report from the front lines (Gabriel Spera's "In a Field Outside the Town," Robert Pinsky's "Samurai Song").

And, as always, there is love—good love and bad (Janet Bowdan's "The Year"), love lost (Paul Perry's "Paris") or thwarted (Rodney Jones's "Plea for Forgiveness"), love recollected (Reetika Vazirani's "Rahim Multani," Donald Justice's "Ralph: A Love Story") and familial (Cathy Song's "Mother of Us All," Charles Fort's "We Did Not Fear the Father") and ever-hopeful (Mark Halliday's "Before"). There is music (Jennifer Grotz's "The Last Living Castrato") and laughter (David Kirby's "At the Grave of Harold Goldstein") in the face of oblivion— yes, the big words are permissible, tangled up as we are in the cusp of the Millennium. Appropriate to the era, there are elegies for the passing of heroes, of good times, and of innocence (Patricia Spears Jones's "Ghosts," Susan Mitchell's "Lost Parrot," Lawrence Raab's "Permanence," Ray Gonzalez's "For the Other World").

If, as Carl Phillips writes, "there is shadow / now, on the water," then what these poets seek to do is not to ignore that shadow but to describe it and the sun that created it. If the act of writing is "to wring the unspeakable from / a silent alphabet" (Erin Belieu, "Choose Your Garden"), we must ask of our poems not what they can be, but, as Rilke asked of the roses, "What can't they be?"

To be or to do: What is the question?

Words are also actions, and actions are a kind of words.
—RALPH WALDO EMERSON, "The Poet"

If we look at the etymology of the word *inspiration,* we see that inspiration is nothing less than the process of inhaling the spirit; the shaman, the griot, the poet are the conduits between the outer and inner worlds, and their medium is the breath upon which words ride. Breath—inhaled, inspired—returns as poetry, as song, as life breathed back into the community. A window opens inside us, and that window opens into the world. Poetry—that sublimely human enterprise—challenges us to pay serious and tender attention both to the things of this world and the journeys of the spirit.

This is where all the arts (poetry, fiction, drama, painting and sculpture, dance and theater and music) meet the humanities (history and biography, sociology and political studies and environmental awareness). But if we look around at the culture we've created, we see that humanities and art have been driven into separate quarters: At first this split seems to be simply a matter of practicality, especially when it comes to endowment grants and the like; but if we follow the line of reasoning used to categorize grants, the separation rapidly grows into a moral impasse. I remember well the deliberations when serving on arts grants panels, where any multidisciplinary proposal ran the risk of being labeled "humanistic"—as if that were grounds for disqualification! Folk art and regional poetry were often categorized under the humanities, which meant that applicants felt compelled to focus on those aspects of the discipline which were popular rather than those which were exceptional and unique. Follow this line of reasoning, and one could easily conclude that the Humanities are meant to serve our sense of community through a catharsis of self-recognition, entertainment, and an easeful delight; whereas Art is demanding, unconcerned with heritage, void of a sense of place, estranged from the everyday, and resistant to social intercourse.

We need only look at the paranoia expressed by some of our political leaders for a hint of where this shuttered thinking leads: The humanities have come under attack for "catering to special interest groups"— as is being argued in the controversy over the history and literature canons; and detractors of the National Endowment for the Arts continue to imply that the arts are "elitist" and narcissistic, self-indulgent. Whenever it is politically opportune, artists are bad-mouthed as hysterical and irresponsible, the perpetrators of a scam to cheat "the people" out of their hard-earned tax dollars. In the last decade of the twentieth century we came to expect such a repressive state of mind from self-righteous "revolutionaries" who cloaked their extremism in patriotic bravado and clichéd chatter of "family values." With their brash simplifications, these self-appointed culture thugs have been progressively successful in jostling the fragile balance of our social and political civility—successful enough, in fact, that they remain a serious threat to civil and artistic liberties into the twenty-first century.

At this critical juncture, it is important to remember that what distinguishes art from commerce is not only the individuals who make the art, but the individual response that art engenders in all of us. Over the past three decades, the National Endowments for the Arts and the Humanities have helped expand the base for the arts and culture in this country so tremendously that the United States has one of the liveliest eclectic arts communities in the world, with a much broader knowledge of the humanities and a more sophisticated audience for culture than before Congress authorized those two exceptional agencies. Federal funding has improved the quality of life for millions in "the pursuit of happiness" by providing access to the very cultural life that was once the privilege of the elite.

Like all artists, we poets cannot afford to shut ourselves away in our separate discipline, honing our specialized tools while the barbarians— no matter if they are religious fanatics or materialistic profitmongers— continue to sharpen their broadswords. Stepping into the fray of life does not mean dissipation of one's creative powers; it may mean less sleep, but it may also mean survival. The reward is a connection on a visceral level with the world as it reshapes its destiny for the new century's countdown.

THE
BEST
AMERICAN
POETRY
2000

◇　◇　◇

Virgin Spring

◊ ◊ ◊

It's a terrible scene, the two men talking to the girl who foolishly lets
    them lead her away
from the road she's taking to church, the men raping and killing her,
    the young boy with them
watching, then left for a while with her body. But the film's next scene
    is more terrible
in some ways, the men and boy arriving at the house where the girl's
    parents live, but not
knowing, and the parents not knowing either, offering a meal, all of
    them sitting together, breaking
bread at a long table—Is that the most awful, or is it when one man
    tries to sell the mother
her murdered daughter's clothes?—and she takes them, pretending to
    consider. Though how
could she pretend at that moment, how control herself? Yet she does;
    she goes outside,
locking them in the barn, and runs to her husband, to whom the task
    of killing them falls.
So it goes on—rape, betrayal, murder, not even the boy is spared. And
    what about the father,
swearing to build a church on the spot his daughter was killed, and the
    miracle of the water
gushing forth from the ground when they lift her body—Is that
    enough, is there some sort
of balance now, good following evil, revenge annulled, the family
    cleansed? What about
the other, dark-haired sister, the pregnant one, who had been a few yards
    behind on the road

to church that morning, who had followed the men and watched from
        a safe distance
while they erased the girl, her prettiness, her spoiled ways, her stupid
        innocence—
I don't know what to make of the sister. She's the one who knows the
        world is brutal
and goes on, scattering seed for the hogs, the one who says nothing,
        the one who survives.

from *Barrow Street*

Semiotics

◇　◇　◇

Rain falls between the notes
the violist in the next apartment plays.
He's one quarter of a distinguished quartet
that hasn't much English; you pass
the same word back and forth. Hello!
What is there to say? The world is dumb
and sings. The world is dumb and speaks
in its big dumb voice that sometimes sounds
like a viola, very nice. Sometimes like diesels. Or
it insists on sign language, waving seasons around
like busy flags. What does it mean that
your heart gets hiccups? The world wants you
to speak its language and you don't know
American Sign or Universal Sign, certainly not
Cosmic Sign. Now your heart wants
an interview. It scribbles madly
on the monitor, giving itself a polygraph test
and failing grandly, proud that it lies.
It never thinks ahead. You're its wrapper,
its bathrobe, and it loves you deeply
but can't remember your name.

from *Boston Book Review*

Shot Glass

◊   ◊   ◊

I'll never forget the day this beautiful woman
right out in the office said I was "sneaky":

I didn't know I was sneaky: I didn't feel
sneaky: but there are mechanisms below our

mechanisms, so I assume the lady was right:
living with that has not helped my progress

in the world, if there is any such thing,
progress, I mean: also it has hurt my image

of myself: I have used up so much fellow-
feeling on the general—all of which I have

forgotten specifically about, as have the
fellows—no offices, no clear images or

demonstrations—I don't understand why that
one remark holds its place ungivingly in me:

and now to talk about it, admit to the world
(my reading public, as it happens) that I am

scarred by an old, old wound about to heal and
about to bleed: this may do confessional good

but I will no longer appear perfect to others:
conceivably, that could be a good thing:

others may be scarred, too, but who wants to
be like them: one should: perhaps I really

do, because lonely splendor is devastatingly
shiny but basically hard and cold, marble

walls and glistening floors: one comfort,
which I am reluctant to relish, is that the

lady is now dead—surely, I am sorry about that,
she was a person of intelligence and

discernment, which is one reason she hurt me
so bad—well, but I mean, she won't hurt

anybody else: she probably did enough good
in her life that the Lord will forgive her:

I am trying to forgive her myself: after all
she left me some room for improvement and

a sense of what to work on. . . .

from *The New Yorker*

Mary Todd
on Her Deathbed

◊ ◊ ◊

I can hear them, choking on spoons, screaming
in shower stalls; the fat are given only
a raw egg and whiskey
                              and those who refuse
to eat are force-fed. The least crazy sing,
picking scalp scabs in window seats.
One woman finds scissors
                              and stabs herself
again and again. It was the tireless Jew
who wore me down; no one believed
that he followed me
                              from train to train
with his satchel of poisons, sneering
as they searched my baggage
for the stolen hotel footstools, how he knew
that I shuffled because my petticoats,
stitched so tight with money,
                              had become a heavy net
for dredging the lost. And I do not speak of the lost:
Abe could have worn me as a boutonniere,
my pinched face, say it: an ugly plump bud,
hoisted skirts and petticoats
                              the leaf and ribbon trim.
I remember the hoisted skirts,
how his body seemed
                              a long white country of its own.

But it was owned by a country
of citizens as unruly as my dead boys,
my dead boys
                    roaring through the White House.
Nothing was mine, after all. Strangers
crowded his open coffin, snipped souvenirs
from the curtains,
                        slipped hands
into the casket to unclip his cufflinks.
All the while, they could hear me
                            wailing from bed.
Every day I can move slightly less;
each body hinge becomes more stubborn
                            than memory.
I know how I will die: a clenched jaw,
fists gripping bed sheets. Stiff with longing,
I will have to break
                        into heaven, the willows
in my handmade girlhood hoop-skirt snapping.

from *Quarterly West*

Choose Your Garden

◇   ◇   ◇

When we decided on the Japanese,
forgoing the Victorian, its Hester
Prynne-ish air of hardly mastered urges,

I thought it would be peaceful.
I thought it would relax my nerves,

which these days curl like cheap gift wrap:
my hands spelling their obsessions; a nervous
tic, to wring the unspeakable from
a silent alphabet.

I thought it would be like heaven: stern,
very clean, virtuous and a little dull—

but we had to cross the bridge to enter
and in the crossing came upon a slaughter
of camellias, a velvet mass-decapitation
floating on the artificial lake,

where, beneath its placid surface, a school
of bloated goldfish frenzied, O-ing
their weightless urgency
with mouths too exact to bear:

    O My Beloved
they said to the snowy
petals and to the pink petals soft as
wet fingers,
        O Benevolent Master

they said, looking straight up at us
where we stood near the entrance, near
the teahouse half-hidden in a copse of gingko,

where even now, discreetly and behind
its paper windows, a woman sinks down
on all fours, having loosened the knot
at the waist of her robe.

        from *TriQuarterly*

RICHARD BLANCO

Mango,
Number 61

◊   ◊   ◊

Pescado grande was number 14, while *pescado chico* was number 12; *dinero,* money, was number 10. This was *la charada,* the sacred and obsessive numerology my *abuela* used to predict lottery numbers or winning trifectas at the dog track. The grocery stores and pawn shops on Flagler Street handed out complimentary wallet-size cards printed with the entire *charada,* numbers 1 through 100: number 70 was *coco,* number 89 was *melón* and number 61 was *mango.* Mango was Mrs. Pike, the last *americana* on the block with the best mango tree in the neighborhood. *Mamá* would coerce her in granting us picking rights—after all, *los americanos don't eat mango,* she'd reason. Mango was fruit wrapped in brown paper bags, hidden like ripening secrets in the kitchen oven. Mango was the perfect housewarming gift and a marmalade dessert with thick slices of cream cheese at birthday dinners and Thanksgiving. Mangos, watching like amber cat's eyes; mangos, perfectly still in their speckled maroon shells like giant unhatched eggs. Number 48 was *cucaracha,* number 36 was *bodega* and mango was my uncle's *bodega,* where everyone spoke only loud Spanish, the precious gold fruit towering in *tres-por-un-peso* pyramids. Mango was mango shakes made with milk, sugar and a pinch of salt—my grandfather's treat at the 8th street market after baseball practice. Number 60 was *sol,* number 18 was *palma,* but mango was my father and I under the largest shade tree at the edges of Tamiami Park. Mango was *abuela* and I hunched over the counter covered with classifieds, devouring the dissected flesh of the fruit slithering like molten gold through our fingers, the pigmented juices cascading from our binging chins, *abuela* consumed in her rapture and convinced that I absolutely loved mangos. Those messy mangos. Number 79 was *cubano*—us, and number 93 was *revolución,* though I always thought it should be 58, the actual year of the revolution—the reason why, I'm told, we live so obsessively and nostalgically eating number 61s, *mangos,* here in number 87, *América.*

from *TriQuarterly*

The Year

◇ ◇ ◇

When you did not come for dinner, I ate leftovers for days. When you missed dessert, I finished all the strawberries. When you did not notice me, I walked four miles uphill past you and into Florence and five miles the other way. When you did not like my dress, I wore it with gray silk shoes instead of gold ones. When you did not see my car had sunk into a snowdrift at the turn of your driveway, I took the shovel off your porch and dug myself out. When you stopped writing, I wrote. When you sent back my poems, I made them into earrings and wore them to work. When you refused to appear at the reunion, I went to the dentist who showed me X-rays of my teeth. When you did not tell me you would be in town, I met you on Main Street on the way to the library. While you had dinner with me, I walked past the window and looked in. You were not there.

from *Denver Quarterly*

Crow Is Walking

◊   ◊   ◊

Crow is walking
to see things at ground level,
the landscape as new under his feet
as the air is old under his wings.

He leaves the dead rabbit waiting—
it's a given; it'll always be there—
and walks on down the dirt road,

admires the pebbles,
how they sparkle in the sun;

checks out his reflection
in a puddle full of sky
which reminds him
of where he's supposed to be,

but he's beginning to like
the way the muscles move in his legs
and the way his wings feel so comfortable
folded back and resting.

He thinks he might be beautiful,
the sun lighting his back
with purple and green.

Faint voices from somewhere far ahead
roll like dust down the road towards him.
He hurries a little.

His tongue moves in his mouth;
legends of language move in his mind.

His beak opens.
He tries a word.

from *Poetry*

Signs

◇ ◇ ◇

when the birds begin to walk
when the crows in their silk tuxedos
stand in the road and watch
as oncoming traffic swerves to avoid
the valley of dead things
when the geese reject the sky
and sit on the apron of highway 95
one wing pointing north the other south

and what does it mean this morning
when a man runs wild eyed from his car
shirtless and shoeless his palms spread wide
into the jungle of traffic into a world
gone awry the birds beginning to walk
the man almost naked almost cawing
almost lifting straining to fly

from *Callaloo*

Man Listening to Disc

◊   ◊   ◊

This is not bad—
ambling along 44th Street
with Sonny Rollins for company,
his music flowing through the soft calipers
of these earphones,

as if he were right beside me
on this clear day in March,
the pavement sparkling with sunlight,
pigeons fluttering off the curb,
nodding over a profusion of bread crumbs.

In fact, I would say
my delight at being suffused
with phrases from his saxophone—
some like honey, some like vinegar—
is surpassed only by my gratitude

to Tommy Potter for taking the time
to join us on this breezy afternoon
with his most unwieldy bass
and to the esteemed Arthur Taylor
who is somehow managing to navigate

this crowd with his cumbersome drums.
And I bow deeply to Thelonious Monk
for figuring out a way
to motorize—or whatever—his huge piano
so he could be with us today.

The music is loud yet so confidential
I cannot help feeling even more
like the center of the universe
than usual as I walk along to a rapid
little verson of "The Way You Look Tonight,"

and all I can say to my fellow pedestrians,
to the woman in the white sweater,
the man in the tan raincoat and the heavy glasses,
who mistake themselves for the center of the universe—
all I can say is watch your step

because the five of us, instruments and all,
are about to angle over
to the south side of the street
and then, in our own tightly knit way,
turn the corner at Sixth Avenue.

And if any of you are curious
about where this aggregation,
this whole battery-powered crew,
is headed, let us just say
that the real center of the universe,

the only true point of view,
is full of the hope that he,
the hub of the cosmos
with his hair blown sideways,
will eventually make it all the way downtown.

from *The Atlantic Monthly*

Between Periods

◇ ◇ ◇

Last night, a friend called
to say she's dying of brain cancer.

Someone is drilling through the still
summer air. The sound clenches
my teeth. It's going in cleanly.
It leaves only a small hole.

My daughter pretends to wash
her hands. As if it were that easy
to wash off the dirt of this world.
She's laughing and wants me
to laugh too, to share the joke
like her first secret.

My friend asked if I was watching
the big play-off game
between my team and her team

before she told me she's dying.
I said *no, I'm watching my kids.*
That must have sounded

a little cold. First time her team's
made the finals. My kids were screaming
about who goes first, who's the leader.

She was hysterical over a hockey game,
suddenly a big fan. We've got some crazy birds

here who start chirping early—not even
close to morning, not a glimmer

of light anywhere. *What the hell is she
doing,* I ask my wife, as if she's to blame.
What the hell is she doing

with cancer? She has a teenage son.
They were watching the game
together. Who's drilling what
on this lazy afternoon? What makes

it lazy? If it's lazy, does that make it
slower for the dying? It's my birthday.
My kids are downstairs making me a crown.

The doctors talked her out of chemo. Too late.
She can still eat. She's lost a lot of weight.
I look good, she said. I didn't know what

to say on the other end.
Oh Debra, Oh Debra, I said
as if repetition could keep her

here. On this earth. I want to be a spike
nailed to it, but it's my birthday—
I'm a stick man with a stick cane.

My son collects sunshine in baskets,
offers me some. I count the states
between us. Will I see her again?
I put on my crown, tilt it
at a jaunty angle. We practice

blowing out the candles. I clean off the Z
on my keyboard. It doesn't get used much.
The A looks great. *Hey kids, let's not answer
the phone, hey kids, let's wash our hands
before we eat.*

She knows what's up. She's keeping
her hair, dyeing it blond,
like she always wanted. *Fuck 'em,*

she said, and started to cry.
It was between periods.
They were going to start up again soon—
she had to go, go, go.

Hope your team wins, I said,
even if it means beating mine.

Fuck 'em, I agreed, and there was nothing
more to say.

I lay sleepless in twisted sheets.
3 A.M. The birds were chirping.
Already? I said.

from *Crab Orchard Review*

The Most Beautiful Word

◇   ◇   ◇

I think "vesicle" is the most beautiful word in the English language. He was lying face down, his shirt burnt off, back steaming. I myself was bleeding. There was a harvest of vesicles on his back. His body wept. "Yaw" may be the ugliest. Don't say, "The bullet yawed inside the body." Say, "The bullet danced inside the body." Say, "The bullet tumbled forward and upward." Light slanted down. All the lesser muscles in my face twitched. I flipped my man over gently, like an impatient lover, careful not to fracture his C-spine. Dominoes clanked under crusty skin: Clack! Clack! A collapsed face stared up. There was a pink spray in the air, then a brief rainbow. The mandible was stitched with blue threads to the soul. I extracted a tooth from the tongue. He had swallowed the rest.

from *Xconnect*

Immigrant Picnic

◇   ◇   ◇

It's the Fourth of July, the flags
are painting the town,
the plastic forks and knives
are laid out like a parade.

And I'm grilling, I've got my apron,
I've got potato salad, macaroni, relish,
I've got a hat shaped
like the state of Pennsylvania.

I ask my father what's his pleasure
and he says, "Hot dog, medium rare,"
and then, "Hamburger, sure,
what's the big difference,"
as if he's really asking.

I put on hamburgers *and* hot dogs,
slice up the sour pickles and Bermudas,
uncap the condiments. The paper napkins
are fluttering away like lost messages.

"You're running around," my mother says,
"like a chicken with its head loose."

"Ma," I say, "you mean *cut off,*
loose and *cut off* being as far apart
as, say, *son* and *daughter.*"

She gives me a quizzical look as though
I've been caught in some impropriety.
"I love you and your sister just the same," she says.
"Sure," my grandmother pipes in,
"you're both our children, so why worry?"

That's not the point I begin telling them,
and I'm comparing words to fish now,
like the ones in the sea at Port Said,
or like birds among the date palms by the Nile,
unrepentantly elusive, wild.

"Sonia," my father says to my mother,
"what the hell is he talking about?"
"He's on a ball," my mother says.

"That's *roll*!" I say, throwing up my hands,
"as in hot dog, hamburger, dinner roll. . . ."

"And what about *roll out the barrels?*" my mother asks,
and my father claps his hands, "Why sure," he says,
"let's have some fun," and launches
into a polka, twirling my mother
around and around like the happiest top,

and my uncle is shaking his head, saying
"You could grow nuts listening to us,"

and I'm thinking of pistachios in the Sinai
burgeoning without end,
pecans in the South, the jumbled
flavor of them suddenly in my mouth,
wordless, confusing,
crowding out everything else.

from *Poetry*

Incest Taboo

◇   ◇   ◇

It always freaked me out when my father
called my mother "Mommy," as in "Mommy,
let's pack up the car and go for a drive!"
I grew up to be afraid of birds.
I swerve now whenever a sparrow swoops
towards my windshield. I can't go to the beach
because of the seagulls that dive and circle
like hornets or warplanes. Even humming
birds creep me out, the way they just hover
quivering like they are about to explode.
Blue jays, robins, even doves have wronged
me, one way or the other. All lousy parrots.

I was changing my bathing suit at the beach
house my parents rented. It was a parrot
green one-piece with a yellow swoop
of daisies down the front. It was wrong
the way my brother Fred barged in—the bird
brain—without knocking, his voice exploding,
"The drive-in starts in two minutes!" He hovered,
my suit rolled down around my hips. "Mommy
wants you to hurry up," he said, leering. The hum
of a car engine out front, my father
honking. Then Fred backed away. My suit left wet circles

on the floor. On the movie screen, explosive
wings and Tippi Hedren. Two clean semi-circles
arched the dusty windshield, a splatter of white bird
poop the wipers couldn't reach. My father

yelled, "Mommy! Look at that! They're running the wrong
way!" Sea water sloshed in my ears, humming,
the soundtrack fading in and out, dialogue swooping
from the crackling gray box hanging from my mother's
window. Fred avoided looking at me. He parroted
bird screeches. His fat greasy hands hovering
over the popcorn made me say, "You ugly beached
whale! Share! . . . Mom and Dad, look, Fred's driving

me to drink!" "That's enough," my father replied, hum-
drum dad-talk, as though the drive-in
was as good a place as any to announce my wrong
turn, to foreshadow my own alcoholism. Beach
bunny Jane, fourteen—that's me—with a father
as good or bad as most, a hovering
mother. Did I know then I'd wind up terrified of birds—
hunched under bar stools, screaming about the parrot
on Baretta's shoulder? The next day I circled
the beach house block on a rusty bike. "My mother's
a bitch," I said, meaning Fred. Freckles exploded
on my arms. My ponytail, a bright chestnut swoop.

Years later, at the party, my husband hovers
over me, trying to control my drinking, swooping
towards each rum and coke, like a father
trying to save the boiler before it explodes,
like a mother bargaining with the beach—
"Give me back my son and I'll be the best mother
in the whole world! I know I was wrong
to let Fred swim alone." She'd trusted that circle
the sun made in the sky, but never again. "Jane drives
herself crazy with regret," my husband says, a parrot
to my whims. The party is humming
with rumors, guests screeching like dawn-inspired birds.

I never wanted to become a mommy.
That is, I wanted to stay sexy, unburdened
by diapers. I wanted to walk a birdless beach
without a string of toddlers behind me, pull-toys humming.
I was sure my body would explode

during childbirth. I dreamt of parrots,
instead of babies, flying through my legs. My father
had wanted a boy, someone he could teach to drive
golf balls into the future, someone he could swoop
down and lift to the basketball hoop, a circle
of victory. He had Fred who hovered
behind him, a cub, until everything went wrong.

I say the same words over and over, a parrot
who wants her Prozac-cracker. My therapist wears the wrong
colors—spring, though she's clearly an autumn. Explosive
dinosaur earrings brush her neck, hover
near her collar. I'm distracted, humming
"The Wind Beneath My Wings," drawing a circle
around each question. "If we'd rented a beach
house, I think I'd remember!" my father's voice swoops.
He reminds me Fred was a good son, a Boy Scout. *The Birds*
is my least favorite movie. "What drive-in?
We never went to any drive-ins," my mother
insists. "I don't like mosquitoes. Just ask your father."

How can I break the incest taboo circling
my own marriage? My husband looks less like my father
when he wears my lingerie. I don't hum
even when he's sick—I won't soothe him like a mommy.
Every girl is part Jane—part me—hovering
around puberty, a sleazy corner. Adults drive
by quickly so they won't remember their imploding
hearts, nothing ever as intense again. Bird-
watching aggravates me. "It's wrong,"
my mother said, talking about *girl* watching, Fred's swooping
eyes scanning breasts and thighs, his mouth parroting
his friends' dirty talk. All winter he waited for the beach.

Baretta's parrot, also named Fred, drives
me to think about that moldy beach
house where Fred picked up my wet suit. His voice hovered
close to my ears. "Everything's related. Parrots
descend from dinosaurs. That's why mommy
is afraid of them," Fred said, swooping

my bathing suit into the air, humming
a Donny and Marie love song. "You're *so* wrong!"
I said, about the parrots with dinosaur grandfathers.
Fred locked my door with a hook that looked like a bird's
beak and flapped his arms like seagull wings, circling
a fish who was me. My insides exploded

as he pushed me on the twin bed, his palm swooping
over my mouth. Now the radio explodes
I'm a bitch. I'm a lover. I'm a child. I'm a mother . . .
trying to shock me with its top ten song, circle
lyrics that make me wish I still had that parrot
green bathing suit that proved my bird-
bee-beeing brother walked in on me, then hovered.
That proved he came in again, after my father
had fallen asleep, dreaming of a walk on the beach
all by himself. I don't think he was wrong
to want out, my mother in the shower, humming.

Fred liked to shoot things, especially birds
which were more challenging than cans. His guns hummed
with promises of taxidermy. Parrot-
sized birds he couldn't name were driven
out of trees and plopped dead in circles
onto the ground. I knew killing was wrong,
even birds, and I'd yell to my mother,
"Make him stop!" She waited for beach-
weather, then buried her son's fun, explosive
pangs of anger in her chest. "You're his father,
talk to him," she said as her husband swooped
his fork to his plate—me crying, silence hovering.

I finally felt happy, though I knew it was wrong.
At Fred's funeral, his girl-watching buddies hovered
near the casket, crying in huddles, circles
football players make before they swoop
and clobber the other team. I was learning to drive.
I'd missed drivers' ed to stand with my father
near the casket. My mother kept fainting, parroting,
"Thanks for coming," to the mourners whose grief exploded

like shaken soda bottles. Sometimes I hear them hum
like I did that summer at the beach
when bottles popped right on 7–11 shelves. A bird-
like cashier. Glass shards. My father yelling, "Look, Mommy!

Look at that!" My father and mother
still don't remember seeing Hitchcock's *The Birds*
or the swooping seagulls. Even the beach house
is caught in a blurry circle of memory, humming
and hovering, ready to explode. It doesn't help
I get details wrong—
Baretta had a cockatoo, not a parrot.

from *Barrow Street*

Birthday

◇ ◇ ◇

I have a confession to make—
When I was young
I was constantly losing shoes.
Of course, the climate was different then:
The trees both bigger and easier to climb,
The birds more virtuous,
More butterflies, fewer clouds,
And all around
The smell of burning peat.
Blue men roamed the earth
Behind stone walls built by Romans
At the far end of our yard
Where the jungles of Southeast Asia began.
You see, I was a legionnaire sent to find the North Pole—
My brother was Horatio Hornblower. . . .
No, we were all away when the zeppelin landed—
My father was magistrate in Khartoum,
Where my mother tended to the sick,
My brother had just befriended Niels Bohr,
When I signed the petition to free Dreyfus.
Mata Hari lived next door—
It was her the zeppelin came for—
Like Baba Yaga she kept a shrunken head
On her front porch, with a lighted candle in it—
We all knew she worked for the other side
And ate Crusader flesh, she was a real pterodactyl.
That was the year the Nile overflowed its banks, that Krakatoa, east of Java,
Sent the reek of burning cloves through the South Seas.
In Siberia a woolly mammoth skull was found,

Under a mountain of ice, on my tenth birthday, my brother was in bed
With scurvy, and rickets, and elephantiasis of the liver, and
My mother gave him balms, and myrrh, and more balms and myrrh,
and mustard plasters, and I got a blunderbuss, a jaguar, and a
troglodyte, and we ate figs and eels and Baked Alaska and drank grena-
dine straight from the bottle, we witnessed the invention of gunpow-
der, and saw gauchos lasso rheas with bolas and drink maté, while
natives buried fish in the garden, with Marco Polo, and Good King
Wenceslaus pummeled Bad King John into submission until he saw
stars—Andromeda and Orion and Draco the dragon—we made him
ride over the Bridge of Assizes with the last of the Hittites on a don-
key, naked through the streets of Coventry, Maximilian brought aard-
vark to the dance, and was summarily executed, by Savonarola, who
stole fire from the gods and tried to get away on the back of a roc, and
then on a juggernaut, only to cause Ragnarök, the twilight of the gods;
it was then, too, that Rasputin danced with Mary, Queen of Scots, for
the last time, I can still see her sobbing into her mantilla.

from *The Germ*

Alpha Images

◇ ◇ ◇

A

In the beginning
God climbed Louis Zukofsky's
pocket step ladder.

B

We see from above
she faces east, her bosom
of the matriarch.

C

No great mystery,
he that rears on one hind leg.
Pegasus' hoof print.

D

Alfred Hitchcock as
pregnant with the devil as
with a certain air.

E

Where is the handle
and what hand stuck this pitchfork
into a snowbank?

F

Stand it on the moon
for a nation of ants, who
know not where they live.

G

Balancing a tray
with one hand, the other hand
poised to pluck the veil.

H

The minimalist's
gate to hell and heaven, these
corridors of light.

I

Blind to what's ahead,
behind, the ego takes this
pillar for a name.

J

Take pity on this
tattered parasol—too chic
for junk or joystick.

K

What looks like a squawk
is to the ear a moth or
butterfly, clinging.

L

Lest we should deny
the ethereal we have
the hypothenuse.

M

Dragging its belly,
a mechanical spider,
its nose to the ground.

N

A scene from Up North
on a postcard, a timber
frozen as it's felled.

O

The rim of the moon.
Peephole into an igloo.
Shadow of zero.

P

How you choose to hold
it determines the weapon.
You may need tweezers.

Q

Might this be the light
at the end of the tunnel,
the visible path?

R

Head, shoulders, and chest—
who's the cameo inside
this dressmaker's bust?

S

Suppose our hero
tore the spent fuse from the stick.
Say the sound of it.

T

Though you can't see what
road you're on, the sign ahead
reads like calvary.

U

More mind than matter
is symmetry's mirror. You
should be that lucky.

V

V is for virgin.
Whether spread or locked, her legs
are the point of view.

W

Symbol of tungsten
and the filament itself,
its light is the white.

X

North—as if a place
as much as idea—four
needles pointing there.

Y

This flower has bloomed,
become so huge as to dwarf
both stem and petals.

Z

Swordplay with air—zip
zip zip—stitches which seem a
bout to disappear.

from *Beloit Poetry Journal*

Walt, I Salute You!

◇　◇　◇

after Pessoa

From the Year Of Our Lord 19★★,
from the Continent of the Amnesias,
from the back streets of Pittsburgh
from the little lit window in the attic
of my mind where I sit brooding and smoking
like a hot iron, Walt, I salute you!

Here we are. In Love! In a Poem!
Slouching toward rebirth in our hats and curls!
Walt, I'm just a woman, chaperoned, actual, vague, and hysterical.
Outwardly, my life is one of irreproachable tedium;
inside, like you, I am in my hydroelectric mode.
The infinite and abstract current of my description
launches itself at the weakling grass. Walt, everything I see I am!
Nothing is too small for my interest in it.
I am undone in the multiplication
of my perceptions. Mine is a life alive with the radioactivity
of its former lives.

I am in every dog and hairpin. They are me! I am you!
All is connected in the great seethe of seeing and being,
the great oceans and beaches of speeding and knowing.

I groan and surge, I long for hatches and engine sumps,
for sailors in undershirts. Walt! You have me by the throat!
Everywhere I turn you rise up insurmountable and near.

You have already been every Conestoga headed to California
that broke down in a cul-de-sac of cannibalism in the Rockies.
You have been every sprouting metropolis rerouted
through three generations of industrialists.
You, the sweat of their workers' brows! You, their hatred of poets!

You have been women! Women with white legs, women with black mustaches,
waitresses with their hands glued to their rags on the counter,
waitresses in Dacron who light up the room with their serious wattage.
Yes! You are magically filling up, like milk in a glass, the white
nylon uniform, the blocky shoes with their slab of rubber sole!
Your hair is a platinum helmet. At your breast, a bouquet of rayon violets.

And you have been places! You have been junkyards with their rusted
    Hoovers,
the pistils of wilted umbrellas.
And then, on the horizon (you have been the horizon!)
Walt, you are a whole small town erupting!
You are the drenched windows. The steaming gutters.
The streets black and slick as iron skillets.
The tawdry buildings. The rooms rented.
And now, in total hallucination and inhabitation, tired of being yourself—
Walt, the champ, the chump, the cheeky—you become me!
My every dark and slanderous thought. Walt, I salute you!
And therefore myself! In our enormous hats! In our huge mustaches!
We can't hide! We recognize ourselves!

from *Boulevard*

Mrs. Hill

◇ ◇ ◇

I am so young that I am still in love
with Battle Creek, Michigan: decoder rings,
submarines powered by baking soda,
whistles that only dogs can hear. Actually,
not even them. Nobody can hear them.

Mrs. Hill from next door is hammering
on our front door shouting, and my father
in his black-and-gold gangster robe lets her in
trembling and bunched up like a rabbit in snow,
pleading, *Oh, I'm so sorry, so sorry,*
so sorry, and clutching the neck of her gown
as if she wants to choke herself. *He said*
he was going to shoot me. He has a shotgun
and he said he was going to shoot me.

I have never heard of such a thing. A man
wanting to shoot his wife. His wife.
I am standing in the center of a room
barefoot on the cold linoleum, and a woman
is crying and being held and soothed
by my mother. Outside, through the open door,
my father is holding a shotgun,
and his shadow envelops Mr. Hill,
who bows his head and sobs into his hands.

A line of shadows seems to be moving
across our white fence: hunched-over soldiers
on a death march, or kindly old ladies
in flower hats lugging grocery bags.

At Roman's Salvage tire tubes
are hanging from trees, where we threw them.
In the corner window of Beacon Hardware there's a sign:
WHO HAS 3 OR 4 ROOMS FOR ME. SPEAK NOW.
For some reason Mrs. Hill is wearing mittens.
Closed in a fist, they look like giant raisins.
In the *Encyclopaedia Britannica Junior*
the great pharoahs are lying in their tombs,
the library of Alexandria is burning.
Somewhere in Cleveland or Kansas City
the Purple Heart my father refused in WWII
is sitting in a Muriel cigar box,
and every V-Day someone named Schwartz
or Jackson gets drunk and takes it out.

In the kitchen now Mrs. Hill is playing
gin rummy with my mother and laughing
in those long shrieks that women have
that make you think they are dying.

I walk into the front yard, where moonlight
drips from the fenders of our Buick Dynaflow.
I take out my dog whistle. Nothing moves.
No one can hear it. Dogs are asleep all over town.

from *The Southern Review*

We Did Not Fear the Father

◊ ◊ ◊

We did not fear the father as the barber who stood
like a general in a white jacket with a green visor cap.
For six long days he held a straight razor like a sword
until his porcelain-chrome chariot became a down-home chair.
The crop-eared son learned to see how the workingman's
day job after the night shift filled the son's small pockets
with licorice, filled the offering plate, and paid for the keeper
who clipped our grape vines under his own pageant.

We did not fear the father as landlord in our three-story tenement
who took charge of four apartments and the attic dwellers.
We searched each corner of the dirt cellar for a fuse box
while he broke out plasterboard upstairs with a sledgehammer.
We peeled out paper from wire mesh and read the headline news
a century old before he lifted us like birds into our bunk beds.

We did not fear the father until he entered the tomb of noise
for his night job, shaping molten steel into ball bearings
as we stared into the barbed grate where he stood
before the furnace sending smoke into the trees.
Fear became the eight-hour echo and glow inside his skull,
the high-pitched metal scraping our ears as our provider
left the factory floor with oil and sawdust inside his mouth
and punched out as fermented daylight burned his eyes.
We did not fear our father until he stooped in the dark.

from *The Georgia Review*

Seven Roses

◊ ◊ ◊

Three red, one white, one purple, one yellow, one pink.
Seven roses in a jar on the kitchen table, the morning
paper, Kona coffee, a plate of sliced melon and banana.
I'm in a fogbank. I was out wandering the keeps
of some mind or another far too late. Now all I can do
is stare at the roses, which smell wonderful, as does
the fruit, as does the coffee. The truth about life is
that it is good, but it comes with a lot of strings attached.
The rosebushes were here when we bought
this house, though we have added to them, subtracted
from them. Frankly, I don't like them much. They
demand so much of you. They want to be fertilized
and pruned and mulched. Then they get sick, they
get rusty and moldy, and things live in them and you
must resort to despicable substances, you have to
wear yellow gloves. All that time out in the heat
when you could be bodysurfing or reading a book.
If I were Rumi I could make a parable about the roses,
I could dance into a fainting spell and someone on my staff
would write down the poem I uttered, or if I were Francis Ponge
I could study the roses in a way that a cubist might,
just before painting them all up and down a stretched canvas.
I've looked at the hard truth: that my heart might be just
too dark for roses. Or my soul too weary. Or my mind
too confused. Yet they *are* beautiful here in their cut
ripeness, their delicate bowing to earth. See how the air
beads into water all along the jar. And the white rose,
its delicate, almost invisible kiss of red at the edges of
its inner petals. It is all so strange in the morning when

I cannot think, and when my body at rest wishes to remain
at rest, which is the law, after all. I know it's the way
of the world that the roses and I have so much to do
with one another. It's one hand washing the other hand.
It's morning, and I take to the day slowly, grow
into my senses slowly. And maybe the roses puzzle after me in
their fashion, the seven lovely roses sitting on my table,
scenting the sunlit room. Maybe they know that I know
how they hate the way they are softly, softly dying for me.

from *The Georgia Review*

And in the Afternoons
I Botanized

◊ ◊ ◊

Where we sat, on the flagstone terrace behind the house,
Gin cooling in the spill of civilian twilight, ice cubes
Doing the dead man's float, with air rough to the touch,
The birch leaves blown yellow, in the lacerating shape of spades,
And thin boughs heaving a little with the season's sickness,
You said: We've come to calamity and the end of things.
Even the bees are weary, and the honey heavy, the petals depressed.
The wars you lose last longer than the wars you win.

And it was true. I could feel the same breeze, pallbearer of the birch,
October heading the dark cortège. Where others might trace
Lifelines in the palm, I read, on the back of my hand,
Liver spots like annotations on a last draft. No goldfinch
Flew to the feeder of wild seed; in the worked earth,
No chipmunk burrowed at the sweet root of the bulb.
And yet, in the mornings, fruit still hung fresh and firm,
Dew-dappled apples, frost smoke thick on the ground.

You said: If that crusty north-of-Boston poet had put us
In a poem, would we stand stiff as figures from a snow globe,
The trees bowed down around us, each branch bent
With the weight of meditation, the cling of imagery? Or would we
Lean on a worm fence, blood stropped in the heart,
Between us those moments where anger rubs on injury—
The tone medium wry, the pace pieced out in syllables
That stick in the throat, the ache of everything unsaid?

Well, better that than chintz and chimes, some teapot dame
Who'd make us talk on stilts, or in the weak repeats of
Rondeaus and rondels, French inventions that sound like
Girl groups from the Sixties. Would you rather lose yourself
In the cold echoes of Eliot, his vaulted voice dry as
Stone commencements at the graveside? Or find yourself
Edged out by the muscle of music in late Yeats?
We'll take our own line, broken, with a grain of sense and salt.

But no words slow down the dirt. And these drinks,
Essence of emptiness from the juniper berry, can't bring back
A duckweb spray of maple paddling in the slipstreams of spring,
Or the flowering crab, or panicles of japonica. You said:
At 47, I'm in my prime numbers, indivisible, entered
Only by myself and one other—odd and middling and absolute—
The mind still testing out every hedge against death,
The short con and the long shot, the bet called on the come.

It's no wonder we nail our days to the wall, and hang
Distractions of the calendar, slick colors over the Xed-out box:
Gaunt barge of Venice in the green canals; the loveknot puzzles of
Women in the pink; and from Monet, the blue and purple pulp of
            waterblooms.
So all our albums fail the past: pictures of picnics and the rose ribbons of
Girls dozy under the summer oak; your unparalleled apparel,
That dress the shade of bittersweet; and my brand-new panama,
Black band around the crown, hat like an elegy for the head.

You said: If we were characters cast in a play, could we choose
Some comedy written in the wit of Restoration, and call ourselves
Lord and Lady Vainhope, or the Fallshorts of a London season?
We'd stumble through contraptions of the plot, dull but not despised,
Wanting only to be better than we were, the axis of laughter
Set spinning by the jibes of gentlemen, the housemaid's joke.
A frump of mangled language, a squire's fat harrumph,
We'd ride out the raillery, redeemed as the footlights dimmed.

It might be worse. The Greeks would strap us both behind
A mask of agony, and raise, behind us both, tall columns
Glazed with gore, history dripping from the choral odes.

I'd rather see myself aggrieved in Italy, young and speaking
Blank verse in the twisted streets, a moonmad lover
Swooning over poison and a toy sword. These days,
They'd heap us unrehearsed in garbage cans, two bums
Practicing their rap before the bottom and the silence fell.

And what had the light left? A Chinese banner of a cloud
Burned across the sun, scarlet and gold of pennants at half-mast,
As the last glow lowered. Strung out among the spikes of dahlia,
A spider's tension stripped the air, a tripwire brushing
The dawdly fuss of a butterfly. You said: Sometimes I feel
Like a rabbit in the brightbeams, or a statue packed in sawdust,
Chained and crated and stowed away. How could I move,
Always made to bear up the dead weight of the self?

In this state of the ladybug and the buckeye whose shell
Battles back the winter like a scaled-down mace, where each
Politician and professor fights for his own empire of ideas,
Theories that colonize the brain, we've reached a common level:
Freaks under the tent, as damaged as Patty the Penguin Girl
Or the Dancing Pinheads, bad goods in the chromosomes, and pain
The price of admission, as the babies know, dangling brow-down inside
            the thighs,
Their first look at the world bloody and the wrong way up.

If we're all born, as Augustine said, between the feces and the urine,
We have a bone to pick with anatomy. And what was *his* problem—
Too much time spent cramped under the pelvic shelf? You can tell,
On every page, his pleasures in confession, nosing out the rank
And the dry rot, the mossy odors of the soul. I'd like to hear him
Alive and in Vienna, knees tucked up on the couch, as the dream doctor
Probed below the belt, fingers wrinkling in his beard: Vell, Herr Augustine,
Vunce more about your mother, and that voice calling from the vall.

Every rebel bred in appointed peace, every child squeezed from
Some squall in the loins, looks on love like a maggot,
That soft surgeon cleaning out the open festers where they hurt.
Who wouldn't sigh to live among the satisfied, in a mansion of
White linen, high polish, white paint, the windows unfolding on
A square of fountains from which the waters leaped in chandeliers?

All those who rise from rags to rages have had their infancy
Where the ends are mean and no gods ease the difficult middle.

You said: It comes clear now, that midsummer month of rain,
And the mushrooms over the lawn, large and limp, spread flat
Like severed ears listening for the next tremor, the resurrection of the flesh.
In the darkness, after the storms, everything sounded too loud, too close.
What could I do? There's only so much the rain can erase,
In natural baptism or new flood. That ooze draining through the night,
That rush and suck of water on the run—it frightened me,
As if heaven once more had breathed into the slippery limbs of mud.

By that stand of asters and the late mallow, where we sat
Like monks gone blind in the margin of manuscripts, and heard
Those arguments whose laws lead to the great Therefore, our hands
Stretched and met, both of us ghostly in the pale stains,
The mineral wastes of moonlight, deep dredge of shadows beneath our feet.
You said: Is there no way out of this helpless evidence?
And I put my shaken fingers to your lips, that wound
The words come from, worn down, drifting, like leaves in a sleepy wind.

from *Parnassus*

For the Other World

◇ ◇ ◇

For those who ran in the streets,
there were no faces to welcome them back.
José escaped and loved the war.

For those who swam with bitterness
of a scorched love,
there was a rusted car to work on.

For those who merely passed
and reclined in prayer,
there was the tower and the cross.

For those who dedicated tongues
to the living and dying,
there were turquoise-painted doorways.

For those who left their children
tied to the waterheater,
there was a shout and a name.

For those whose world
was real and beautiful,
there was a cigarette and a saint.

For those who asked José
to stay and feed his children,
there were flowers at their funerals.

For those who carried a shovel
tattooed on their backs,
there was a wet towel and a bottle.

For those who swept the street
of superstition and lie,
there was the turquoise house to come home to.

For those who came home late
and put their swollen feet up,
there was love and the smell of dirty socks.

For those who feared the devil
and spit on his painted arms,
there was a lesson in rosaries.

For those who had to leave
before the sun went down,
there was asphalt and a bus.

For those who stared at wet plaster
and claimed the face of Christ appeared,
there was confinement and stale bread.

For those who talked with each other
and said it was time to go,
there was lead in the paint and on the tongue.

For those who left children behind,
there was a strange world
of sulphur and sparrow nests.

For those who accused their ancestors
of eating salt, there were these hands
tracing what was left after the sweat.

from *Crab Orchard Review*

JENNIFER GROTZ

The Last
Living Castrato

◇　◇　◇

Difficult to believe, a knife insures the voice,
soprano notes proceed intact while chest hair and beard
accompany the new lower octaves, the voice expanding

beyond sex, limited only by lung. And now whole
operas composed for castrati are abstract and
unperformable, now whole species of off-humans who

were sacrificed for air, for air sinking and rising
in their throats, are extinct, now facsimiles
reproduce for our ears what is digital mastery,

bleeding soprano and counter-tenor. Except for
the brief miracle of Edison's recording:
the last living castrato's voice brimming through

static and hiss. Technology at its beginning and
old school opera at its decline, that cusp
between where a voice spanning five octaves sang

to give us proof of the voice, and of how
we doctored it to make it more whole, to widen
emotion's aperture. He held it

in his mouth. Audiences would beg for
the aria to be sung over and over,
interrupting the story, which was only

an excuse for the voice. The voice is *how,*
rising, rising, so as to dive,
and he held it in his mouth releasing

our cruel sacrifice, our gratitude
to hear it fall, driven to where
the voice takes us: silence, applause.

from *New England Review*

The Dump

◇ ◇ ◇

He died, and I admired
the crisp vehemence
of a lifetime reduced to
half a foot of shelf space.
But others came to me saying,
we too loved him, let us take you
to the place of our love.
So they showed me
everything, everything—
a cliff of notebooks
with every draft and erasure
of every poem he
published or rejected,
thatched already
with webs of annotation.
I went in further and saw
a hill of matchcovers
from every bar or restaurant
he'd ever entered. Trucks
backed up constantly,
piled with papers, and awaited
by archivists with shovels;
forklifts bumped through
trough and valley
to adjust the spillage.
Here odors of rubbery sweat
intruded on the pervasive
smell of stale paper,
no doubt from the mound

of his collected sneakers.
I clambered up the highest
pile and found myself
looking across not history
but the vistas of a steaming
range of garbage
reaching to the coast itself. Then
I lost my footing! and was
carried down on a soft
avalanche of letters, paid bills,
sexual polaroids, and notes
refusing invitations, thanking
fans, resisting scholars.
In nightmare I slid,
no ground to stop me,

until I woke at last
where I had napped beside
the precious half foot. Beyond that
nothing, nothing at all.

from *The Threepenny Review*

Before

◇   ◇   ◇

Before you were *you*,
before your bicycle appeared under the street-lamp,
before you met me at the airport in a corduroy jacket,

before you agreed to hold my five ballpoint pens
while I ran to play touch football,
before your wet hair nearly touched the piano keys

and in advance of how your raincoat was tightly cinched
when you asked about nonviolent anti-war activity
and before you said "Truffaut,"

before your voice supernaturally soft sang
"I aweary wait upon the shore,"
before you suddenly stroked my thigh in the old Volvo,

when you had not yet said "Marcus Aurelius at 11:15"
and before your white shirt on the train,
before Pachelbel and "My Creole Belle"

and before your lips were so cool under that street-lamp
and before Buddy Holly in Vermont on the sofa
and Yeats in the library lounge,

prior to your denim cutoffs on the porch,
prior to my notes and your notes
and before your name became a pulsing star,

before all this
ah safer and smoother and smaller was my heart.

from *Xconnect*

Ode to
the Lost Luggage Warehouse
at the Rome Airport

◊ ◊ ◊

Until you've visited the lost luggage warehouse
    at the Rome airport in August, you have not lived,
the Mediterranean sun insinuating itself
    into the inner sucking marrow of your bones,
roasting your epidermis like a holiday bird.
    A goose, upon reflection, would be the fitting
analogy. You hear the faint sizzling of the fat
    under your skin, organs grilling, brain singed
as you walk to the guardhouse and show the uniformed
    sentinel your paper that certifies you have indeed
lost your bag. You gaze at his amazing hat with plumes
    tinted maroon and gold while he scrutinizes your clutch

of ragged forms, signed by Signor Nardo Ferrari,
    minor functionary with the state airline
at the *ufficio* in Florence, who has confided
    in beautiful English he will retire at the end
of the month and devote himself to the cultivation
    of vegetables and fruit, a noble endeavor,
but you suspect he'll not be leaving his lush *paradiso*
    to iron out your petty problems, for you have come
in pursuit of your bag, supplicant on a holy quest to retrieve
    that which is your own, or was once your own,
the dresses, coat, boots, and intimate et cetera,
    nothing priceless, no treasures as such, but dear to you,

especially the black coat you bought in Paris
　　in a decrepit building below Sacré-Coeur,
going with Mimi after lunch, giving the secret password,
　　hearing the answering hiss, walking up four flights
of stairs to a room filled with ugly clothes,
　　one divine coat, now lost in the dark regions
of this Italian underworld, you hope, for if not here,
　　it's apparently nowhere, and this warehouse is a warren
of high-ceilinged rooms with thousands of bags stacked
　　on metal shelves, precariously piled backpacks
with scurf from Katmandu, Malmö, Khartoum, Köln, Kraków,
　　Istanbul, Reims in France or Francia in *italiano,*

chic makeup cases, black bags like the suitcases of doom,
　　hard-shelled portmanteaus like turtles (soft parts
incognito, mating in tandem), briefcases, carpet bags,
　　19th-century trunks with straps and buckles,
and you see a woman, *molto dolorosa,* in latex gloves,
　　a surgeon delving, methodically, in a suitcase
filled with Japanese snacks—arare, dried squid, rice candy
　　wrapped in thin edible paper, red and green jellied
sweets—recognized from your childhood in Hawai'i, and amid
　　the *conglomerazione* of heat, memory, and rage you imagine
a Japanese man, thinking, I'm going to Italy, but the food,
　　I'll hate it, then packing his favorites: the sublime

shredded mango of blessed memory, cracked plum, dried peas,
　　and you think of Sei Shōnagon, supercilious court lady
in 10th-century Japan because you are reading her Pillow Book,
　　a record of things that disgust or please her
and you whip your kimono around and say,
　　"Things I adore about Rome: the lingerie stores
for nuns with their fifties bulletproof brassieres
　　and other medieval undies; the floor of St. Peter's
with its imperialistic measurements of the lesser cathedrals
　　of the world, St. Paul's in London, the Milan cathedral;
Caravaggio's *Bacchus* and *Madonna of Loreto.*
　　Things that disgust me in August: backpacks with cheese,

child carriers imbedded with the scum of mashed
    bananas and cereal, petroleum-laced breezes
from jet exhaust, the color navy blue." Your Italian
    is meager but the denizens of this particular realm
of hell are courteous if lethargic and show you
    that the bags are stacked by month:
agosto, luglio, giugno, but that's as far
    as they go. No Joe DiMaggio or before. To be
anywhere else is all you want. You hate your clothes,
    no coat's worth the flames licking your feet, but
you take a careful waltz through the months,
    and find nothing in the midst of so much.

The whole long way back to Florence, while the gorgeous
    panorama of the countryside flies by,
you have a *caffè,* try to read, but a few seats down
    a child screams, hysterical with fatigue,
and you see his face with its sticky impasto of snot,
    candy and tears, and you think of all your losses,
those past and the ones to come, your own death,
    il tuo morto, which makes the loss of a French coat,
shoes, and a few dresses seem ridiculous.
    You think of your arrival in Florence, the walk home
from the station past the Duomo, your husband's hands,
    his kisses and the dinner you'll eat, prosciutto

and melone, perhaps, some ravioli in a restaurant
    near the Sant'Ambrogio market, you'll buy a new coat
for winter, an Italian coat, *il soprabito,*
    one more beautiful than the one lost. That's the way
your life will go, one day after another,
    until you begin your kamikaze run toward death.
It makes you sick to think of it until you begin
    to get used to the idea. I'd better get busy,
you think, enjoy life, be good to others,
    drink more wine, fill a suitcase with arare,
dried squid because when you leave home anything can happen.
    You may be caught in a foreign country one day,

without money, clothes or anything good to eat,
    and you'll have to try that stinky ravioli,
brine-soaked pig knuckles, poached brains quivering
    on a wooden platter, tripe, baked ear wax,
fried grasshoppers, ant cakes, dirt soufflés,
    and though it seems impossible, they could prove
delicious or at the very least nourishing,
    so don't make a fool of yourself, and one day
you may join Signor Ferrari in his bosky Eden.
    Everyone will be there God, Jesus and Mary,
your mother and father, even your pain-in-the-ass sister
    who got everything. Heaven, you hate it:

the conversation's boring, and everyone's so sane,
    so well-adjusted. And it's cold. Heaven should be warm,
a bit like Tahiti, so you're furious, and then you see
    your sister, and she's not cold because she's wearing
your French coat, but you're not in heaven, you're on a train,
    going faster, it seems, as you approach Florence.
You're in a muddle, glum, have nothing to show
    for your day but a headache and a blister
on your heel. You want the train to crash,
    blow you to kingdom come. You want your mother
to kiss you, call you Baby, Darling; you'd sell
    your soul for some shredded mango or dried plum.

from *Five Points*

Goldsboro Narratives

◇   ◇   ◇

GOLDSBORO NARRATIVE #4:
MY FATHER'S VIET NAM TOUR NEAR OVER

The young dead soldier was younger
than they thought: the 14-year-old passed
himself as seventeen, forged
a father's signature. In the army no more
than months, he was killed early
the week before a cease-fire.
The boy was someone-I-somewhat-knew's
older brother and someone-my-mother-
had-taught's son, and, lying
in the standard army casket, an American
flag draped over the unopened half,
the boy didn't look like anyone
anybody would know—a big kid his dark skin
peached pale, lips pouted. I was sure
I didn't recognize him.

            When kids older than us
closed down one campus after another,
I thought they'd close all colleges down,
and there would be no place for me
when it was my time. It didn't seem fair.

            Capt. Howell's wife answered
the door one day, and two men
in military dress asked to come in.
She had no choice, I suppose,

but once they came into her living room,
she no longer had a husband, and
the three boys and the girl no longer
had their father. *So this is how
it happens,* I thought: two men come
to your house in the middle of the day,
ringing a bell or rapping on the door.
And, afterwards, there's nothing left
to look forward to.

GOLDSBORO NARRATIVE #7

Time was a boy, specially a black boy,
need to be whipped by his kin, teach him
not to act up, get hisself killt.
Folks did this cause they loved them boys.
The man laughs. And boys would do what all
they could to get out of them whippings,
play like they was getting tore up,
some play like they was going to die.
My grandmama the first one that whipped me,
and she made me get my own switches.
If I came back to her with a switch too small,
she made me go right back and get a big one.
And she whipped me for that, too. He laughs.
I loved that woman, though. Sho did.

GOLDSBORO NARRATIVE #28

When folks caught on to what was happening
between Rev. Johnson and Sister Edna,
the grown-ups went back to speaking
in front of children as if we couldn't spell.
It was easy to figure out, though:
Rev. Johnson's wife didn't get happy; and,
after service, she wouldn't shake hands
with Sister Edna or any of her kin.
And Sister Edna's husband, Mr. Sam,

who never came to church, began waiting
in the parking lot to drive his wife home.

Now the age Rev. Johnson was then, I doubt
he was concerned with being forgiven.
But when I was 12 and kept on falling
from available grace, I began dismissing him
and mostly all of what he said he meant.
I went witnessing instead to Mr. Sam,
his truck idling outside the paned windows,
him dressed in overalls and a new straw hat.

from *Callaloo*

Air for Mercury

◇   ◇   ◇

I.

After the double party
for the poorly loved

when the gleam in the hound's eye
fell like glass rain on the south

lawn of the countergarden, when
the images of false flags sank

in the mirrored plaques,
when the mirrored plaques

had been passed in, they took
your days and gave them back,

before you unsnapped first
the crenellated shoulder wings

then the fumbling then the little
ankle wings and sent them back

to the wing patrol, in the box,

in the metal box, in the genital
mouth of the rose (the open forms

of the state left so
undone that you were stranded

on the nonimperial coast having
a boat unnamed for you)

you were free, you were
having a bout of meaning

II.

A leaf hurried by on its
side. Of what is knowledge made?

A season stopped by without your
noticing, saying, lost file, breath boy;

the sun had leaked its power
into things, and all notation had

become inaccurate suddenly, you'd been trying
to talk to them from this

coast, you'd been trying to help
them in their small groups

III.

Monsters of will and monsters of
willessness confront the garden; a dragon

crow greets the dusk with its
prow. Rhyming is a tool of

friendly desperation. The spirits will return
though they're not here now.

IV.

Oracles, iron, the misuse of fire
under the young earth, and this

business of being infinitely swept up
in possibility so when you put

your hand down on something white
you noticed that detail, punctuated by

luckless forms. But night had been
deployed: see-through parts of the moon:

lace, anima mundi; and weren't there
two forevers, words and space, between

which more *experience* might ride, unencumbered?
You were supposed to tell them

what they'd missed; they'd read your
logics, your letters. So little space

between your letters, the words couldn't
easily air themselves. Remember going back

and forth between the rooms? Blue,
green; the wings had been adjusted.

You were meant to take black
netting off a face or two. Take

something. Passion brought you
here; passion will save you.

from *Boston Review*

Considering the Demise
of Everything

◊   ◊   ◊

What if the 5:30 train shaking the trees at the edge of the woodlot—
What if the yellow flowers blooming in the swamp—
What if I can't find what I'm looking for?
Then thank you. Thank you water and pen, bell and candle.
Thank you rope, your coarse length lowers me
Into the mineshaft. Cobalt and copper and diamond.
Thanks for the hammer. And the canary.
The bird is grateful for the opportunity to sing,
Its yellow feathers fluffed at the neck.
Its song a bituminous flame, like a match
Struck deep in a cavern. Is that water ahead?
Is that a ladder? Thank you for the cross-hatched
Sky and the days I was able to
Lie down under it with the man I loved.
What if it's summer and the clouds are gondolas?
What if I'm led beside still waters and cannot rest?
My head on his chest, looking up at the sky
While he combs the bangs off my forehead.
The sky is a handpainted clock.
Sometimes sun, sometimes moon.
The cross-hatching is accomplished by the terminal
Ends of branches. It's the library lawn.
It's the town square of a small southwestern city.
Two old men playing checkers in the gradual dark.
Speaking Spanish across the courtyard: *rampido rampido.*
Who will translate? We are done with traveling.

We are hot and the last time we bathed was two states ago,
A creek just after sunrise. We are so thirsty.
And nothing is better than this water, this canteen.
This drinking.

from *Harvard Review*

Epistle

◇ ◇ ◇

We want the operation because we want the cure.

We are naked and open unto his eyes, though draped in antiseptic linens. He is quick and powerful, piercing even to the dividing of soul and spirit, though both choose amnesia. He separates them, even as he divides the joints and marrow, discerning the thoughts and intents of the heart in a small, vestigial, rooted, and determined thing.

Later, he shows how the sick part was woven in, by lacing the middle finger of his right hand, his knife hand, among the fingers of his left. He found it, severed it, stitched closed the wound it left, then backed out of the larger wound, shutting each layer behind him. An eye tips each of his bloody fingers.

There was that instant when the anesthetic took hold, and some triviality—the chrome rim of a lamp—slipped from focus. Our eyes clung to the slippery shine. Then, not even the darkness they entered registered.

So the cut came, the skin parted, the fat, the muscle, the membranous sheaths, the different colored layers, all doused in bright oxygenated blood, which was expertly sprayed away, so the invasion would be clear.

But first the skin was shaved, then painted with antiseptic, the tomb jewel color of ochre, liberally applied. First the diagnosis was made. First the protocol and the procedure were recommended. We wanted the operation because we wanted the cure.

First the morning that we woke with a new unease that did not fade by lunchtime. First the night we could not sleep, as sleep kept cracking underfoot. First the hand of a companion, asking, "Are you all right?" First our own voice answering, saying, "I don't know." And the voice that stated frankly, "No, you're not."

Thus God performs his surgery, closing and opening simultaneously, always with new reasons to go in.

from *Meridian*

Ghosts

◇ ◇ ◇

He was filled with beauty, so filled he could not stop the shadows
from their walk around his horn, blasting cobwebs in the Fillmore's ceiling

Somewhere dawn makes up for the night before, but he is floating.
Dead in the water. And yet, my lover tells me, he saw him shimmering.

As did others. It could have been the *acid*. Or fragmented harmonics.
His reed ancestral. This perilous knowledge. The band went home,

shivering. A girl threw roses in the water. Carnations, daisies. And bright red
        sashes.
Like ones the Chinese use for funeral banners. A drummer intoned chants

from the Orient. Police wrote up the news. Years later, my lover told me
Friends would hear the whisper, then a tone, full throttle from the wind.

Ghosts on Second Avenue, jazzmen in the falling stars.
If you catch one, your hands will glitter.

from *Crab Orchard Review*

Plea for Forgiveness

◊   ◊   ◊

The old man William Carlos Williams, who had been famous for kindness
And for bringing to our poetry a mannerless speaking,

In the aftermath of a stroke was possessed by guilt
And began to construct for his wife the chronicle

Of his peccadilloes, an unforgivable thing, a mistake
Like all pleas for forgiveness, but he persisted

Blindly, obstinately, each day, as though in the end
It would relieve her to know the particulars

Of affairs she must have guessed and tacitly permitted,
For she encouraged his Sunday drives across the river.

His poems suggest as much; anyone can see it.
The thread, the binding of the voice, is a single hair

Spliced from the different hairs of different lovers,
And it clings to his poems, blond and dark,

Tangled and straight, and runs on beyond the page.
I carry it with me, saying, "I have found it so."

It is a world of human blossoming, after all.
But the old woman, sitting there like rust—

For her, there would be no more poems of stolen
Plums, of round and firm trunks of young trees,

Only the candor of the bedpan and fouled sheets,
When there could no longer have been any hope

That he would recover, when the thing she desired
Was not his health so much as his speechlessness.

from *The Atlantic Monthly*

Ralph: A Love Story

◇   ◇   ◇

In what had been a failing music store
A man named Flowers opened the first cinema
In Moultrie. Ralph was the projectionist,
At seventeen the first projectionist.
And there was an old upright from the store
On which the wife accompanied the action
With little bursts of von Suppé and Wagner.

Ralph liked the dark of the projection booth;
He liked the flickering images on the screen.
And yet because he liked it all so well,
He feared expulsion from this little Eden,
Not so much feared as knew the day must come,
Given his luck, when it would all run out,
Which made the days more paradisal still.

Margot, the daughter, twenty and unmarried—
To tell it all quickly—seduced Ralph.
She let him think he was seducing her.
They used to meet in the projection booth,
Embracing wordlessly but laughing too,
Unable to suppress their self-delight.
Time after time they had been almost caught.
Then, as in novels, Margot became pregnant.

Sundays the cinema was closed.
                                    Ralph packed
And slipped off to the depot about dusk.
That evening from the train he watched with a certain nostalgia

The sparse pale farmlights passing from his life—
And he understood nothing, only that he was young.
Within a week or two he joined the navy.

Not that he realized it at the time,
But those quick laughing grapplings in the dark
Would be the great romance his life would know,
Though there would be more women, more than he wanted
Really, before it was all finished for him.
And even in the last few years, working
His final job, night watchman at a warehouse,
He would be resting on a stack of lumber,
Toward morning, say, and there would come to him
The faces of the stars before the stars
Had names, but only dark-painted eyes and hands
That spoke the sign-language of the secret heart.
(Oh, not that he remembered, he did not.)

She wrote him over the first months two letters
In care of his parents in another town.
The envelopes were decorated boldly
With home-drawn hearts, some broken, pierced by arrows.
And the mother must have guessed the truth and thought
To spare the son by keeping back the letters
Until the time seemed ripe for him to have them.
And when his tour of duty ended finally
He did unseal and read them and was sorry.
But he could not go back to it, he could not.

So it was gone, the way a thing will go
Yet keep a sort of phantom presence always.
He might be drinking with some woman, lying
Beside her on a tourist cabin bed,
When something would come ghosting back to him,
Some little thing. Such paradise it had been!

And when it *was* all finished for him, at the end,
In the small bedroom of his sister's house,
Surrounded by his shelves of paperbacks—
Westerns mostly, and a few private-eyes—

Lying there on the single bed, half gone
On Echo Springs, he could not call it back.
Or if it came back it was in the form
Of images in the dark, shifting and flashing,
Badly projected, spooling out crazily
In darkness, in a little room, and he
Could not control it. It was like dying.
No, it *was* dying, and he let it go.

from *The New Criterion*

Six Apologies, Lord

◇ ◇ ◇

I Have Loved My Horrible Self, Lord.
I Rose, Lord, and I Rose, Lord, And I,
Dropt. Your Requirements, Lord. 'Spite Your Requirements, Lord,
I Have Loved The Low Voltage Of The Moon, Lord,
Until There Was No Moon Intensity Left, Lord, No Moon Intensity Left
For You, Lord. I Have Loved The Frivolous, The Fleeting, The Frightful
Clouds. Lord, I Have Loved Clouds! Do Not Forgive Me, Do Not
Forgive Me LordandLover, HarborandMaster, GuardianandBread, Do Not.
Hold Me, Lord, O, Hold Me

Accountable, Lord. I Am
Accountable. Lord.

Lord It Over Me,
Lord It Over Me, Lord. Feed Me

Hope, Lord. Feed Me
Hope, Lord, Or Break My Teeth.

Break My Teeth, Sir,

In This My Mouth.

from *The Antioch Review*

DAVID KIRBY

At the Grave
of Harold Goldstein

◊　◊　◊

I'm at a graveside service for someone I didn't know,
          a Mrs. Goldiner, the mother of my friend Maxine,
who is sitting with her sisters, Jill and Andrea
          and sniffling a little as the rabbi, who calls himself
"Rabbi" when he phones the house, as in
          "This is Rabbi" ("Don't you think that's primal?"
Maxine will say later. "Don't you expect someone
          with a robe and a staff in his hand?"),

is saying how the dead woman grew up in Pennsylvania
          and went to New York and worked for Saks Fifth Avenue
and met her future husband at a party, and by now
          I'm daydreaming in sepia about the Lower East Side
and anxious first-generation immigrant parents
          and yeshiva boys and pigtailed girls in gingham dresses
and storefronts and pushcarts and Model-A Fords,

when suddenly I realize that I'm standing by the grave
          of someone I *did* know, Harold Goldstein, who was
the dean of the library school at the university
          where I work and whom I liked a lot, a person
"of pure character," as his headstone says, and,
          continuing with the engraver's characteristic disregard
of punctuation, "lofty aims/life rich in generous
          regard for others, and devotion to publicity,"

and I think, Well, that's one thing we had
        in common, and then I look again, and of course
it says, "devotion to public duty," not publicity,
        and for a moment I blush to think not only
of my exaggerated self-love but also my eagerness
        to associate myself with someone as fine as
Harold Goldstein, who, as far as I could tell,

was pure, lofty, generous, and so on,
        whereas I, even in my late forties, am different
only in degree rather than kind from
        the self-appointed j. d. of *annum domini* 1961,
tough-guy-in-his-own-mind-only
        who had but dreamed of genuine juvenile democracy,
dreamed of being bad enough
        to be sent by his parents to all-boys Catholic High,

which was part religious school and part
        minimum-security detention center, since it contained
not only the sons of the faithful but also
        most of the fuck-ups from the public schools,
who were now concentrated under one roof
        and therefore in a position to learn additional vices
as well as pass on the ones they had already mastered

to such a one as I, who would digest far more
        of the world's nastiness were he to be yanked summarily
from the cookies-and-milk milieu of Baton Rouge High
        and set down without preamble among the brawlers,
purse snatchers, serial masturbators, and teen alcoholics
        of dear old CHS, one of whom was the inestimable
Riley Tucker of this narrator's youth, which Riley,
        having revealed his penchant for crime even earlier,

had been sentenced to terms in Catholic
        Elementary as well as Catholic Junior High
and by now was specializing in the theft,
        joyriding in, and abandonment of General Motors
vehicles—the bigger, the better, since his ordinary mode

of transport was not only shamefully legal
but small, a Renault with the engine in the back

and a two-tone town-and-country horn
        that his father had given up for the Buick
that better matched his position in life,
        whereas the Renault only mocked Riley's outlaw status;
worse, one of the conditions of his sentence
        was that he had to take his sister to
her all-girl school, St. Agnes, which she had
        to attend as a parallel to Riley's incarceration,

though eventually he persuaded his mom to alternate days
        with him so we could join the track team, our workouts
consisting less of stretching and running laps and more
        of eating Hershey Bars and drinking Seven-Ups and smoking
Riley's supply of shoplifted Chesterfields and Kools.
        This one day I needed a ride home,
so after school I set out with Riley in the Renault,

and when we got to St. Agnes, the girls were waiting
        out front, most of them having undone the top buttons
of their blouses and pulled their plaid skirts up
        and laid out on the lawn to enjoy the last of the sun
while they waited for their rides and listened to
        the ineffectual cluckings of the elderly nun
whose job it was to see them off the premises,
        and what happened next was that Riley

decided to "cut some maneuvers" in the Renault
        so the girls could see how fabulous we were,
only, in the course of the zigs and the zags
        and the zips, Riley spun the wheel so hard
that we found ourselves on the wrong side
        of the little French car's notoriously high center
of gravity, and we ended upside down in the parking lot,

the Renault teetering nicely on its roof as Riley
        and I huddled on our heads and shoulders and watched
Riley's sister get in their mother's car—where did *she* come from?—

and vanish. Standing at the grave of Harold Golstein,
I can still see Riley's upside-down mother
        giving us a single disgusted glance and then
driving away slowly, her car gliding as though fixed
        to some futuristic monorail.

Suddenly there is a commotion: Rabbi has alluded to the fact
        that Maxine's sister Andrea is pregnant
by her husband Charles, only Andrea too has been daydreaming
        and thinks Rabbi has said "her husband Al,"
who is actually Maxine and Jill and Andrea's late father,
        so Andrea says, "Charles! Charles!" and the others say,
"Rabbi said, 'Charles,' Andrea," and Andrea calms down.

What was Riley's mother doing at St. Agnes anyway?
        Obviously either she or he had got the day wrong,
but I'll never know, because the totaled Renault
        was towed and forgotten, and I,
guilty by association, walked everywhere for a year,
        though usually down to the corner,
where I waited for Riley to come by in his latest acquisition,
        the theft of which I was also an accessory to,

I suppose, even if we were never caught. My crimes are
        little ones these days, but I guess we should all
do the best we can, so it's probably good to have
        this kind of accident, by which I mean the unplanned
rediscovery of a person like Harold Goldstein,
        of which the world needs more, not less,
and whose example I have resolved to emulate

as much as my below-average character and mediocre aims
        permit, even though his way, the right-side-up way,
is not especially aesthetic, but why even think about
        aesthetics when things are falling apart all around you
and death and misunderstanding are on every side?
        Then again, in *Stardust Memories,* when Woody Allen
asks these wise space aliens who visit Earth
        if he shouldn't be performing more good deeds,

they tell him that if he really wants to serve humanity,
      he should tell funnier jokes—wait, that's *my* duty,
I think, that's my public duty! Because sooner or later,
      we all turn upside down: you're zipping along nicely,
a hot-shot, and everybody's checking you out, when boom,
      over you go. And look! There goes your mother!
She's driving away slowly across the ceiling of the world.

from *Parnassus*

The Oration

◇　◇　◇

after Cavafy

The boldest thing I ever did was to save a savior.
I reached heights of eloquence never achieved before
Or since. My speech turned the mob around!
They lifted the rood from his back, they dropped to the ground
Their nails and flails. But the whole time I spoke
(It's a wonder it didn't throw me off my stride)
The prophet or seer or savior, whatever you care to call him,
Kept groaning and muttering, telling me to be silent.
He was mad of course, so I simply ignored him. Poor fellow,
The beating they had given him must have turned his wits.

Every ounce of persuasion it took to convince the crowd
In the powerful sun, including the priests and his followers,
Exhausted me utterly. When I was sure he was safe,
The ungrateful fellow! I took my way home and collapsed
On my cushions with chilled wine. Then, I heard later,
The savior harangued the mob with outrageous statements
That roused them to fury anew: he denounced the priesthood
As corrupt; he pronounced himself king of the world;
He said God was his father. So they strung him up again.

A violent thunderstorm woke me to a sky full of lightning
So I rushed out in the rain, forgetting my cloak,
And found him dead and alone except for a handful of women
Weeping and carrying on. Well, it taught me a lesson,

To mind my own business—Why, the crowd might have turned on me!
Still, I have to be proud of my eloquence.

                                                It was the speech of my life.

from *The Threepenny Review* and *Poetry Daily*

The Muse of the Actual

◊   ◊   ◊

She'd hate if her mother were proved right—
that having her, he'd never leave his wife.
We were sitting on the back deck, looking
at the apple trees, that had fluttered white
a week ago, but now were green and plain.

We blew our black tea cool while she told me
the other day he'd sat where I was sitting,
to paint the hill, the trees, and, so she would
think of him each time she looked, a bull,
pawing a fallen apple in the foreground.

I guess you could call it a self-portrait,
she laughed, and went laughing to get it
from her bedroom, then propped it against
the deck rail in the shade of the grape trellis
so we could sit looking back and forth

from the painted hill to the actual,
identical except for the bull, who did
resemble him, hunched forward, restless.
He does that, she said after a while.
Sort of paws around. I mean with me.

She swirled her tea and sipped.
Sometimes it's like he's still painting.
Smudging things. His tongue
working away like a brush—his tongue
and other things. I keep thinking

I should ask if he sees me as fallen.
A sigh. *The truth is I like being*
the muse. He hadn't painted for years.
Now love had restored his desire.
Her own desire was never so intense

as in the moment he drove off again,
back to the wife in Ithaca. *Talk about*
myth, she said. I stared at the bull,
half expecting it to turn into him,
burst from the canvas, wild with love

for her and willing to forsake the world
to prove it. But I knew the world
was closer to her mother's version.
Whatever the miracles of art, the bull
would stay put, like the laws of the actual.

from *The Southern Review*

The Goddess
of Quotas Laments

◊   ◊   ◊

George Wallace is dead.
Few recant as he did, dropping
Skeins & masks, but I still see
The army of dragon's teeth

He planted like Cadmus of Tyre.
Fists of oaks clutch barbed wire.
How many replicas of him relume,
Wheedling east & west, here

To Kingdom Come, in vernal
Valleys & on igneous hillocks
That overlook god knows where?
I wish I knew why hatemongers

Drift to the most gorgeous
Spots on earth. I have watched
Choke vines & sunlight in cahoots,
Edging toward a cornered begonia.

from *TriQuarterly*

THOMAS LUX

Henry Clay's Mouth

◊   ◊   ◊

Senator, statesman, speaker of the House,
exceptional dancer, slim,
graceful, ugly. Proclaimed, before most, slavery
an evil, broker
of elections (burned Jackson
for Adams), took a pistol ball in the thigh
in a duel, delayed, by forty years,
with his compromises, the Civil War,
gambler ("I have always
paid peculiar homage to the fickle goddess"),
boozehound, ladies' man—which leads us
to his mouth, which was huge,
a long slash across his face,
with which he ate and prodigiously drank,
with which he modulated his melodic voice,
with which he liked to kiss and kiss and kiss.
He said: "Kissing is like the presidency,
it is not to be sought and not to be *declined.*"
A rival, one who wanted to kiss
whom he was kissing, said: "The ample
dimensions of his kissing apparatus
enabled him to *rest* one side of it
while the other was on active duty."
It was written, if women had the vote,
he would have been President,
kissing everyone in sight,
dancing on tables ("a grand Terpsichorean
performance . . ."), kissing everyone,

sometimes two at once, kissing everyone,
the almost-President
of our people.

from *The Atlantic Monthly*

LYNNE MCMAHON

We Take Our Children
to Ireland

◇ ◇ ◇

What will they remember best? The barbed wire
still looped around the Belfast airport,
the building-high Ulster murals—
but those were fleeting, car window sights,
more likely the turf fires lit each night,
the cups of tea their father brought
and the buttered soda farls, the sea wall
where they leaped shrieking into the Irish Sea
and emerged, purpling, to applause;
perhaps the green castle at Carrickfergus,
but more likely the candy store
with its alien crisps—vinegar? they ask,
prawn cocktail? Worcestershire leek?
More certainly still the sleekly syllabled
odd new words, gleet and shite,
and grand responses to everyday events:
How was your breakfast? Brilliant.
How's your crust? Gorgeous.
Everything after that was gorgeous,
brilliant. How's your gleeted shite?
And the polite indictment from parents
everywhere, the nicely dressed matrons
pushing prams, brushing away their older kids
with a Fuck off, will ye? Which stopped
our children cold. Is the water cold,
they asked Damian, before they dared it.

No, he said, it's not cold, it's
fooking cold, ye idjits.
And the mundane hyperbole of rebuke—
you little puke, I'll tear your arm off
and beat you with it, I'll row you out to sea
and drop you, I'll bury you in sand
and top you off with rocks—
to which the toddler would contentedly nod
and continue to drill his shovel
into the sill. All this will play on
long past the fisherman's cottage and farmer's
slurry, the tall hedgerows lining the narrow
drive up the coast, the most beautiful
of Irish landscapes indelibly fixed
in the smeared face of two-year-old Jack—
Would you look at that, his father said
to Ben and Zach, shite everywhere, brilliant.
Gorgeous, they replied. And meant it.

from *The Southern Review*

The Hours of Darkness

◇　◇　◇

When there are words
waiting in line once more
I find myself looking
into the eyes of an old
man I have seen before
who is holding a long white cane
as he stares past my head
talking of poems and youth

after him a shadow
where I thought to see a face
asks have you considered
how often you return
to the subject of not seeing
to the state of blindness
whether you name it or not
do you intend to speak of that
as often as you do
do you mean anything by it

I look up into the year
that the black queen could still see
the year the the alien lights
appearing to her and then going
away with the others
the year of the well of darkness
overflowing with no
moon and no stars

it was there all the time
behind the eye of day
Rumphius saw it before
he had words for anything
long before he wrote
of the hermit crabs *These*
wanderers live in the houses
of strangers wondering
where they had come from
Vermeij in our time
never saw any creature
living or as a fossil
but can summon by touch
the story of a cowrie
four hundred million years old
scars ancestry and what
it knew in the dark sea

there Borges is talking
about Milton's sonnet
and Milton hears the words
of Samson to someone else
and Homer is telling
of a landscape without horizons
and the blind knight whom no one
ever could touch with a sword
says in my head there is
only darkness
so they never find me
but I know where they are

it is the light
that appears to change and be many
to be today
to flutter as leaves
to recognize the rings of the trees
to come again
one of the stars is from
the day of the cowrie

one is from a time in the garden
we see the youth of the light
in all its ages
we see it as bright
points of animals
made long ago out of night

how small the day is
the time of colors
the rush of brightness

from *Poetry*

Lost Parrot

◇   ◇   ◇

She can cry his name from today to tomorrow.
She can Charlie him this, cracker him that, there
in the topmost he hangs like
a Christmas ornament,
his tail
a cascade of emeralds and limes.

The child is heartsick. She has taped messages
to the mailboxes, the names
he responds to, his favorite seeds.
At twilight she calls and calls.

Oh, Charlie, you went everywhere with her,
to the post office and the mall, to the women's
room at the Marriott where you perched
on the stall, good-natured, patient.

And didn't you love to take her thumb
in your golden beak
and, squeezing tenderly, shriek and shriek
as if your own gentleness
were killing you?

You were her darling, her cinnamon stick, her pedagogue.
You knew her secret names
in Persian and Greek. At the beach
you had your own chair and umbrella.
Oh, pampered bird. The neighbors sympathize. But what's

love compared with wild red fruit, a big
gold moon, and an evening that smells of paradise?

If she were older, she'd join the other
sad girls for drinks, she'd lick
the salt from her tequila glass and say something wise
she'd heard said a hundred times before.
Love is a cage she's glad to be free of.

Oh, Charlie, you were her pope and popinjay, her
gaudy, her flambeau, her magnificat.
You were the postcard
each morning delivered to her room, her all-day sunset.

In the topmost fronds you squall and squawk
to the other flashy runaways.
Say paradise! No dice, no dice.

from *The Atlantic Monthly*

Aunt Lily
and Frederick the Great

◇   ◇   ◇

After the war, she painted her walls
a French blue, pale as the watered
blue silk of her eyes, filled her rooms
with cream and gold-leaf chairs,
and when she raised her porcelain cup
with pinky arched and blew the word
"Limo-o-o-gges" across the lip,
that made a tender wind, as if a host
of cherubs rafted through the room.
Mad for all things French,
she'd never read Voltaire,
went straight from the Academy
of Typing in the Bronx to work
for Mr. Hyman at the J.D.C.
In 1945 she went to Paris—ah, the city
was a shambles then, American cigarettes
were currency, her Yiddish
far more useful than her French
in working with the refugees. History
was hell, she learned, but life
moved on. She purchased
silver fruit knives, teacups, pastel
figurines, and tottered home on platform
wedgies to attend the rattle and attack
of morning trucks along Third
Avenue and to receive us kindly

when we came to call—in short,
to lead a life not *sans souci*
(for there were deaths,
and loneliness), but of her own
design. You'd never guess
King Frederick and my aunt
would have so much
in common. Both were short,
bilingual, stubborn, confused,
enlightened in some ways, benighted
in others, tyrannical, clever, benevolent,
fierce. Like Frederick, she flourished,
like Frederick, she died. She was tiny
and great and is buried in Queens.

from *The Gettysburg Review*

Work

◊ ◊ ◊

1.

I am a woman sixty years old and of no special courage.
Every day—a little conversation with God, or his envoy
    the tall pine, or the grass-swimming cricket.
Every day—I study the difference between water and stone.
Every day—I stare at the world; I push the grass aside
    and stare at the world.

The spring pickerel in the burn and shine of the tight-
    packed water;
the sweetness of the child on the shore; also, its
    radiant temper;
the snail climbing the morning glories, carrying
    his heavy wheel;
the green throats of the lilies turning from the wind.
This is the world.

Comes the hunter under the red leaves;
come the hounds, on their stubbies;
like wind they pour through the grass,
like wind they pour up the hill;
like wind they twist and swirl in the long grass.

Every day—I have work to do:
I feel my body rising through the water
                not much more than a leaf;

and I feel like the child, crazed by beauty
            or filled to bursting with woe;
and I am the snail in the universe of the leaves
            trudging upward;
and I am the pale lily who believes in God,
            though she has no word for it,

and I am the hunter, and I am the hounds,
and I am the fox, and I am the weeds of the field,
and I am the tunnel and the coolness under the earth,
and I am the pawprint in the dust,

I am the dusty toad who looks up unblinking
and sees (do you also see them?) the white clouds
in their blind, round-shouldered haste;

    I am a woman sixty years old, and glory is my work.

2.

The dreamy heads of the grass in early summer.
In mid-summer: thick and heavy.
Sparrows swing on them, they bend down.
When the sparrow sings, its whole body trembles.

Later, the pollen shakes free.
Races this way and that way,
like a mist full of life, which it is.
We stand at the edge of the field, sneezing.
We praise God, or Nature, according to our determinations.

Then the grass curls or breaks, or we cut it.
What does it matter?
Do you think the grass is growing so wild and thick
    for its own life?
Do you think the cutting is the ending, and not, also,
    a beginning?
This is the world.

The pink globes of the peonies
open under the sun's early-morning hands.

The vine of the honeysuckle
perks upward—
the fine-hold of its design
did not need to be so wonderful, did it?
but is.

This is the world.

The bat squeaks.
The bat leans down out of dark July
with his elf's face.

The twenty-winged cloud of yellow butterflies
floats into the field.
The mustard-heads bend under their soft weight.

This is the world.

3.

Would it be better to sit in silence?
To think everything, to feel everything, to say nothing?
This is the way of the orange gourd.
This is the habit of the rock in the river, over which the water pours
    all night and all day.
But the nature of man is not the nature of silence.
Words are the thunders of the mind.
Words are the refinement of the flesh.
Words are the responses to the thousand curvaceous moments—
    we just manage it—
    sweet and electric, words flow from the brain
    and out the gate of the mouth.

We make books of them, out of hesitations and grammar.
We are slow, and choosy.
This is the world.

4.

All day I have been pining for the past.
That's when the big dog, Luke, breathed at my side.
Then she dashed away then she returned
in and out of the swales, in and out of the creeks,
her dark eyes snapping.
Then she broke, slowly,
in the rising arc of a fever.

And now she's nothing
except for mornings when I take a handful of words
and throw them into the air
so that she dashes up again out of the darkness,

like this—

this is the world.

5.

The green pea
climbs the stake
on her sugary muscles.

The rosy comma of the radish
fattens in the soil.

Farmers call to the white oxen, together they pull the plow.
Girls sigh upward against the bodies of young men.
The century plant opens at last in the frail moonlight.

6.

And how shall we speak of love
except in the splurge of roses, and the long body
    of the river
shining in its silk and froth;

and what could be more wonderful
than the agility and the reaching of the fingers of Hannah,
who is only seven days old;

and what could be more comforting than to fold grief
like a blanket—
to fold anger like a blanket,
with neat corners—
to put them into a box of words?

7.

It may be the rock in the field is also a song.
And it may be the ears of corn swelling under their
   green sleeves
are also songs.
And it may be the river glancing and leaning against
   the dark stone is also a deliberate music.

So I will write my poem, but I will leave room for the world.
I will write my poem tenderly and simply, but
   I will leave room for the wind combing the grass,
for the feather falling out of the grouse's fan-tail,
   and fluttering down, like a song.

And I will sing for the bones of my wrists,
   supple and exemplary.
And the narrow paths of my brain, its lightnings and issues,
   its flags, its ideas.
And the mystery of the number 3.

I will sing for the iron doors of the prison,
and for the broken doors of the poor,
and for the sorrow of the rich, who are mistaken and lonely,

and I will sing for the white dog forever tied up in the orchard,
and I will sing for the morning sun and its panels

of pink and green on the quiet water,
and for the loons passing over the house.

I will sing for the spirit of Luke.
I will sing for the ghost of Shelley.
I will sing for the Jains and their careful brooms.

I will sing for the salt and the pepper in their little towers
    on the clean table.
I will sing for the rabbit that has crossed our yard
    in the moonlight,
stopping twice to stamp the cold ground
    with his narrow foot.

I will sing for the two coyotes who came at me with
    their strong teeth
and then, at the last moment, began to smile.

I will sing for the veil that never lifts.
I will sing for the veil that begins, once in a lifetime,
    maybe, to lift.
I will sing for the rent in the veil.
I will sing for what is in front of the veil, the
    floating light.
I will sing for what is behind the veil—
    light, light, and more light.

This is the world, and this is the work of the world.

from *The Southern Review*

I Do Not

◇ ◇ ◇

"Je ne sais pas l'anglais."
—GEORGES HUGNET

I do not know English.

I do not know English, and therefore I can have nothing to say
about this latest war, flowering through a nightscope in the
evening sky.

I do not know English and therefore, when hungry, can do no more
than point repeatedly to my mouth.

Yet such a gesture might be taken to mean any number of things.

I do not know English and therefore cannot seek the requisite
permissions, as outlined in the recent protocol.

Such as: May I utter a term of endearment; may I now proceed to
put my arm or arms around you and apply gentle pressure;
may I now kiss you directly on the lips; now on the left tendon
of the neck; now on the nipple of each breast? And so on.

Would not in any case be able to decipher her response.

I do not know English. Therefore I have no way of communicating
that I prefer this painting of nothing to that one of something.

No way to speak of my past or hopes for the future, of my glasses
mysteriously shattered in Rotterdam, the statue of Eros and

Psyche in the Summer Garden, the sudden, shrill cries in the streets of São Paulo, a watch abruptly stopping in Paris.

No way to tell the joke about the rabbi and the parrot, the bartender and the duck, the Pope and the porte-cochère.

You will understand why you have received no letters from me and why yours have gone unread.

Those, that is, where you write so precisely of the confluence of the visible universe with the invisible, and of the lens of dark matter.

No way to differentiate the hall of mirrors from the meadow of mullein, the beetlebung from the pinkletink, the kettlehole from the ventifact.

Nor can I utter the words science, seance, silence, language and languish.

Nor can I tell of the arboreal shadows elongated and shifting along the wall as the sun's angle approaches maximum hibernal declination.

Cannot tell of the almond-eyed face that peered from the well, the ship of stone whose sail was a tongue.

And I cannot report that this rose has twenty-four petals, one slightly chancred.

Cannot tell how I dismantled it myself at this desk.

Cannot ask the name of this rose.

I cannot repeat the words of the Recording Angel or those of the Angel of Erasure.

Can speak neither of things abounding nor of things disappearing.

Still the games continue. A muscular man waves a stick at a ball. A
woman in white, arms outstretched, carves a true circle in space.
A village turns to dust in the chalk hills.

Because I do not know English I have been variously called Mr.
Twisted, The One Undone, The Nonrespondent, The Truly
Lost Boy, and Laughed-At-By-Horses.

The war is declared ended, almost before it has begun.

They have named it The Ultimate Combat between Nearness and
Distance.

I do not know English.

from *The American Poetry Review*

Paris

◊ ◊ ◊

after Celan

Make me bitter.
Count me among the almonds.
Drink
From my mouth.

Count me among the almonds.
The night is the night.
From my mouth,
You almost would have lived.

The night is the night.
In the swell of wandering words.
You almost would have lived.
Without words, too.

In the swell of wandering words.
You fill the urns and feed your heart.
Without words, too.
Under the angels.

You fill the urns and feed your heart.
And I lie with you, you in the refuse.

Under the angels,
Twelvemouthed.

And I lie with you, you in the refuse.
Get drunk and name yourself Paris.
Twelvemouthed.
As if we could be we without us.

Count me among the almonds.
Make me bitter.
You almost would have lived.
Make me bitter.

from *Callaloo*

"All art . . ."

◇ ◇ ◇

Routinely the sea,
unbuckling, out-
swells the frame it will

return to, be
held restively
by.

If there is a shadow
now, on the water, if
there are several,

somewhere are those that must
cast them, they will not
stay,

what does?
Our bodies, it turns out,
are not flutes, it

is unlikely that
God is a mouth with nothing
better to do than

push a wind
out, across us,
but we are human,

flawed therefore and,
therefore, shall suit ourselves:
Music

Hard Master
I called out,
Undo me, at last

understanding how
gift, any difficult
knot is—by

fingers, time, patience—
undone, knowing
too the blade by which

—if it means
the best, the most fruit—oh,
let the limbs be cut back.

from *Boulevard*

Samurai Song

◇　◇　◇

When I had no roof I made
Audacity my roof. When I had
No supper my eyes dined.

When I had no eyes I listened.
When I had no ears I thought.
When I had no thought I waited.

When I had no father I made
Care my father. When I had no
Mother I embraced order.

When I had no friend I made
Quiet my friend. When I had no
Enemy I opposed my body.

When I had no temple I made
My voice my temple. I have
No priest, my tongue is my choir.

When I have no means fortune
Is my means. When I have
Nothing, death will be my fortune.

Need is my tactic, detachment
Is my strategy. When I had
No lover I courted my sleep.

from *The New Yorker*

History & Bikinis

◇ ◇ ◇

My favorite uncle would put the chickens to sleep
       by hiding their heads
under his armpit, then rocking them back and forth

       like squalling infants
in his anchor-and-heart tattooed arms while crooning some wordless
       lullaby, before

he chopped their heads off on the oak's scarred stump. "That way
       they never know
a thing," he said. He showed me history in the annual rings

       of that blood-soaked stump.
After he'd plucked the brazen, sun-flecked feathers,
       gutted the carcass,

intestines hot between his fingers, thrown the slop bucket
       to the hogs, and given
the trussed body, obscenely white, to my mother,

       he'd start counting
the outer rings and work his way slowly
       towards the center.

"1963, a good year, plenty of rain, see how wide
       the growth ring is—
'I Want to Hold Your Hand' sold a quarter million copies

in the first three days,"
and then, as an afterthought, "When the monk Trich Quan Duc
burned himself alive

on a Saigon street, the Catholic generals called it
'Buddhist barbecue.'
In our own Birmingham's Sixteenth St. Baptist Church

bombing, four black girls
got killed while the Sunday-school class discussed
'The Love That Forgives.'"

History's synonym is irony. But I, whose body had been jolted
awake by the electroshock
of hormones flooding my brain cells, who was more interested in jerking off

over the Sears & Roebuck catalogue's
lingerie section in the tool shed that reeked new-mown grass,
sperm, and gasoline,

didn't get it. It was all trivia to me, even
when he explained 1952,
Korea, how he had escaped more four-hour mortar attacks by writing

long panegyric letters
to the Russian consulate. "They hustled me out of Seoul
real quick." He tilted

his head and winked. When he saw he'd lost me,
my uncle, who knew
all history backwards, Sorbonne on the GI Bill, but couldn't

pull his shell-shocked life together
and wandered Europe for the next ten years before returning to the States
to stay with us, would stop,

rip open a cloudless blue pack of Gauloises, and light
a cigarette whose smell meant
Paris, boulevards, women, the life I fantasized

as a dirt-poor preacher's
kid in Kansas. Acrid smoke kick-started my uncle's reiterated
hacking, someone turning over

the ignition of a car whose cold engine wouldn't
catch. "Listen,"
he continued, "July 5th, 1946, the bikini bathing suit

created by Louis Réard
made its 'debut' during a fashion show at the Molitor
Pool in Paris. Model

Micheline Bernardini wore the abbreviated outfit,
covered with a newspaper-print
design. I bet you didn't know that the bikini got its name

from the Pacific atoll
where, four days earlier, the U.S. had exploded another
A-bomb?" He nearly

died laughing, "She must have been a bombshell," and went on counting out
the rings until
the great shade tree became a sapling.

Uncle couldn't
stop, kept talking to himself alone, forgot me
in his frantic countdown

that went back before the acorn dropped
and sprouted,
to the Great Fire of Rome and further back,

before the Year Zero
of Our Lord and Savior Jesus Christ, before God's sperm begot
upon a virgin

history, her shrieks and moans that have lasted
two millennia and more,
back beyond Xenophon and his Greek mercenaries crying,

"Thalassa, Thalassa,"
back to Heraclitus whispering, "No god or man has made
this world, which is

the same for all; but it was ever, is now, and ever shall be
an ever-living Fire,
with measures kindling and with measures going out." I left him

raving by the stump
whose green, invisible, burning branches he could never
put out or cut down.

"He's off his rocker" was my mother's official
diagnosis.
"If he stays, I go!" she told my father. All

I can remember clearly
of that summer was the heat and how desire drew me
into the cool darkness

of the tool shed, where I would fumble
with our Sears
& Roebuck bible, turning the pages wildly past

Good Year
radial tires, skillsaws, workboots, ball-peen hammers, Burpee's
sunflower seeds, until I found

the sweet forbidden flesh of the Swimsuit Section between
Hardware and Household.
I would imagine Micheline Bernardini in the world's

first bikini,
and as I came in shuddering spurts onto the oil-soaked rag
my father used to wipe

our Chevy's dipstick clean, everything got mixed up. In the seven seconds
of blinding orgasm, I saw
her sundered flesh, the mushroom cloud rising almost one mile

　　　　　out of the ocean,
ecstasy's alpha and omega, ground zero, a young Japanese
　　　　　girl kneeling, and the dead

chickens running in circles without their heads, chased
　　　　　by my uncle who will
always ask me what the newsprint on her torn, stripped-off bikini said.

　　　　from *Shenandoah*

Kunitz Tending Roses

◇ ◇ ◇

Naturally he doesn't hear too well,
so that when he's kneeling he's really
listening at the very mouth of the flower.
And the feeling in his hands, his sense
of touch, seems gloved if not quite gone,
though when he bleeds he takes a certain
notice, wipes it away, then moves on.

And winter eyes. The old have passion's
winter eyes, which see with a pointillist
chill clarity, but must look close, as his do,
petal by petal, since the work is tactile
visual: Cadenza, Blaze, Red Fountain climbing
or like free-standing rhododendron,
sunset gold Medallion, scarlet Maiden.

His body bends depending on the height
and cluster or, on a perfect scale, the stature
of the rose, which, like the day, declines
continually: meaning that toward evening
he almost disappears among the fragrance,
gala, and double flesh of roses: or when
he's upright, back to the sun, is thin

enough to see through, thorn and bone.
Still, there he is, on any given day,
talking to ramblers, floribundas, Victorian
perpetuals, as if for beauty and to make us
glad or otherwise for envy and to make us

wish for more—if only to mystify and move us.
The damasked, dusky hundred-petaled heart.

Interrogate the rose, ask the old,
who have the seminal patience of flowers,
which question nothing, less for why we ask:
Enchanter, Ember, Blood Talisman, something
to summarize the color of desire, aureate
or red passion, something on fire to hold
in the hand, the hand torn with caring.

from *Poetry*

Permanence

◊　◊　◊

I can't remember how old I was,
but I used to stand in front
of the bathroom mirror, trying to imagine
what it would be like to be dead.
I thought I'd have some sense of it
if I looked far enough into my own eyes,
as if my gaze, meeting itself, would make
an absence, and exclude me.

It was an experiment, like the time
Michael Smith and I set a fire in his basement
to prove something about chemistry.
It was an idea: who I would
or wouldn't be at the end of everything,
what kind of permanence I could imagine.

In seventh grade, Michael and I
were just horsing around
when I pushed him up against that window
and we both fell through—
astonished, then afraid. Years later

his father's heart attack
could have hit at any time,
but the day it did they'd quarreled,
and before Michael walked out
to keep his fury alive, or feel sorry for himself,
he turned and yelled, I wish you were dead!

We weren't in touch. They'd moved away.
And I've forgotten who told me
the story, how ironic it was meant
to sound, or how terrible.

We could have burned down the house.
We could have been killed going through
that window. But each of us
deserves, in a reasonable life,
at least a dozen times when death
doesn't take us. At the last minute

the driver of the car coming toward us
fights off sleep and stays in his lane.
He makes it home, we make it home.
Most days are like this. You yell
at your father and later you say
you didn't mean it. And he says, I know.

You look into your own eyes in a mirror
and that's all you can see.
Until you notice the window
behind you, sunlight on the leaves
of the oak, and then the sky,
and then the clouds passing through it.

from *The Virginia Quarterly Review*

The Beach
at Falmouth Heights

◊　◊　◊

Summer, 1952

All the way from Boston to the Cape my daughters cry:
Today! today!
    and:
        Oh, I see a cow that you don't see!

One or the other is therefore always on the very edge
And poking from the backseat past my husband's face
Or mine a plump pale grubby finger. A shrill voice blows
Out the windows of our nearly new, four-door, blue Desoto:
Liar! liar! pants on fire! I saw Bossy first.
                I think at first
Of Hansel's bony finger, the witch's disappointed wish. . . .
I think of my foolish awkward brother still lost in Korea,
Almost two years since he missed the boat in Hungnam. . . .

There is no mooly cow, I say, *so no one saw her first.*
There is! they cry, *there is!*
             But already we are past
So I ask, *Where?* and they point, both at once.
                  There, there!

My husband drives—wishing, I guess—how am I to know?—
Wishing to be somewhere else again, another world, a war

Away from us. The girls and I—or I—try to inspect
The space around us.
                    The first rule is that there's no there there.
Like Philadelphia, my husband never says. Or Oakland . . .
Milton, Randolph, Brockton, Buzzards Bay. So much scrub,
So much greenery, so little traffic, so much small-town delay.
If I look at him, he shrugs. Who? I want to ask, Who? Who?
Who is she? Who? I sound in my head like the unwise owl.
Can he remember who she was? I'd never ask. I wouldn't dare
His legal expertise, his not-quite-smiling cross-examination.
So I repeat myself.
                    My dears, there's no there there.
No here here. Almost the last of June. Nineteen-fifty-two.
Blue flax in an empty pasture, barbwire strung like a melody
From stave to stave around another prospect of disuse.

She does too exist, they say. *We saw the cow. We saw her.*
Prove it.
        We saw her!
                    But that's no proof at all.
But we saw her!
            I saw a ghost at the piano last night.
No you didn't!
            You mean you *can say you saw a thing*
And you should *be believed, but I . . .*
                            Oh, Mother, Mother . . .

What they have seen is possible, what I have seen is . . .
Their father smiling, smug and safe inside his vow of silence,
Parting us till death, and then . . .

                            Crossing the bridge at Bourne,
High above the bright canal, the little boats, the hard water,
We meet the Cape's cold fog, the promise of unwanted rain.

                        ★★★★★★★

Of course it rained. A gray unpleasant sticky little drizzle.
For two days I played keano for pennies with the old ladies
In the lobby of the Oak Crest Inn, and George took the girls

For rides. Good at taking girls for rides, for stuffed quahaugs
And corn on the cob and ice-cream cones. Good at ruining
Their appetites for dinner. He said he took them clamming.
They spent their mornings watching chambermaids make beds
And in the afternoon they talked about how difficult I am.

★★★★★★★

Will the sun come out? they ask.
It always has.
Or has it?
Yes, I am difficult and so distracted I lose my weight in pennies.

★★★★★★★

The sun came out. In its course. The sand grew bright and hot,
The water like a dance of knives, too cold at first, and then
Just right, so cool, such a pleasure for the Cape's forsaken skin.
My daughters cried because the sand was hot, because
The tide went out, because the fiddler crab played his best tune
On the big claw that bites small children, so my daughters cried. . . .
George consoled them, wrapped them in his meaty arms and legs,
Dried them with the towel, sang to them that lovely song—
Good night, Irene . . .
Irene, good night . . .
I'll see you in my dreams. . . .

★★★★★★★

George went back to Boston, leaving us the summer and the car.
My crocodile daughters cried, of course, when we dropped him
At the station, and stopped the instant his train pulled out.
Little hypocrites. Or do they just forget more readily than I?

Drive Desoto to the beach! the sirens sang. *The beach!*

And I? I understood, for I'd been reading Bishop Berkeley—
Another George!—and so I understood, had always understood,
How George could disappear so thoroughly the girls might come

148

To think he had been no more than the dim idea of God.
Like Martha's Vineyard across the sound, a haze on our horizon.

★★★★★★

All afternoon I watch the old ladies from the Oak Crest Inn,
Card sharpies transported by their gaudy bathing costumes back
To a more brilliant age. Like the debutantes we all would be—
In yards of frilly calico, rubber wading slippers, daisied caps—
To the sea's music they descend the long staircase to the sea,
The long gray weathered rickety steps through the bayberries
And the salt spray roses. Rampant and pink, red and wild,
Each lady makes the summer progress of a widowed queen, while I . . .
I am the youngest dowager-in-waiting, awaiting the last word
From One Who—who knows?—cannot exist except perhaps
Through the pale fawning eyes, the hungry skin of a woman
Who is not me today. George is George today, the answer
To another woman's prayers, the pair of them cupped
In the imaginary hands of the God Who Is . . .
                              never angry enough.
Poor brother Hansel—if he's alive, he's in a Chinese cage.
Father's in hell. Mother's in New Hampshire. George is in love.
And thus I have invented deadmen's fingers, goosefish and God.

Like circus elephants the widows tiptoe into the splintery sea,
Through the tiny breakers, over the stone tulips, to bob
Above their tutus on the shallow wash.
                              Handstands.

                                        Applause
And sympathetic laughter. And the water's famous soothing fingers,
The first touch and probably the last.
                              On the yellowed sheets
Of her deathbed, read the obituary in the BOSTON HERALD,
Her maid found a puddle of Lethe, the waters of forgetfulness.

Janet holds out a devil's-pocketbook, a baby skate for me
To wonder over, and Ellen has the shell of a horseshoe crab,
And both at last have the names I had forgotten because . . .

I remember because I see them now in prayerful attitude
Examining the salty relics of other creatures' canceled lives.
I see on their shoulders the wet tendrils of their brown hair,
So like their father's, and the skirts of their swimsuits clinging
To their plump tan thighs.

What heartbreakers you are to be!

I sigh. I remember. I laugh. I forget. And I cry. Easy as pie.
Bishop Berkeley and my own George were wrong of course,
As wrong as wrong could be. I never heard my daughters cry
That last time.

Mother, pay attention. Look, Mother. See.

★★★★★★★

I looked for mackerel and scup, silversides and common killifish.
I looked away and they were gone, caught, both, in the weave
Of the sustaining sea, carried off, laughing and tumbling
like little shells turning over in the backwash of the merry tide . . .

. . . Or I saw them go, a wave at a time, singing as they sailed
The sun-blind waters to a harbor safe from my imagination.
Silent. Where the dead live. And I shall never want to be.

What was there to tell George, so busy with his life and laws?
So happy that Mister Truman had said he would not run.
George liked Ike, bald and bland as any new-born child.
George saw nothing missing, never has and never will, living
Always in the ever-present moment of an unexamined life. . . .
Each rose-scented day a perfect summer at the beach
Where the siren has no song to sing. Nothing left to tell
George had not heard from the least tern or the laughing gull.
Still . . .
     to settle for *being* when those we loved are gone . . .

from *Black Warrior Review*

Au Pair

◇　◇　◇

The first thing she'd noticed, as they sat her down for lunch
by the picture window, was flags all doing a dance
in front of houses: was today a holiday?
No, they said smiling, it's just the American way,
and she couldn't help reflecting that in France
nobody needed reminding they were French,

but the neighborhood had turned out very nice,
no fences, big yards, kids racing back and forth;
you could let the shower run while you were soaping
or get ice from a giant refrigerator's face.
She couldn't believe how much the franc was worth
and she had no boyfriend yet, but she was hoping,

and because her father was the world's best baker
she naturally thought of his bakery in the Alps
whenever they passed her a slice of their so-called bread,
and sometimes she wished she could hire a jet to take her
back just for breakfast, but as her great-aunt had said
so wisely more than once, it never helps

to make comparisons, so she mostly refrained.
She couldn't believe, though, how here whenever it rained
the mother sent children out without their coats,
not carelessly, but because she had no power
and nobody made them finish the food on their plates
and bedtime was always bedtime plus an hour,

so au pairs were useless really, except for the driving.
Yes, that was puzzling: after she cracked up the car
they didn't blame her or ask her to pay a thing,
but once she let Caitlin eat some sort of cherry
with red dye in it, and then they *were* angry, very.
Americans were strange, that much was clear:

no penmanship, and lesbians held hands
on the street, and most women carried a pair
of pumps in a bag they never took out to wear;
it was so disrespectful, she couldn't understand
how older ones got called nothing, not even Madame,
but then nobody in this country had a last name

which was going to make it hard to write them a letter
when she got back. It was really bittersweet
her visa was running out; she was sad that all
she'd done with her days off was go to the mall,
she'd bought a million T-shirts and that was great
but she had to admit it, saving would have been better,

and she knew somehow that when she got on the plane
she'd probably never live anywhere foreign again
which filled her American family with more pity
than she felt for herself, because at least she was coping,
she'd work at her sister's shop and stay in the city
where she had no boyfriend yet. But she was hoping.

from *Poetry*

Welcome to Ithaca

◇　◇　◇

Since *metaphor* derives from *transferring*
a burden from one to the other, it
was clear, then, from the beginning,
that blood-drenched hall, that it would be easier
to silence pleas for mercy
if heard as the unintelligible
chirping of birds—easier
to string servant girls up like pigeons.
So, Odysseus's heart was a *dog,* its hackles
rising when he saw the women caught up
in the suitors' arms, someone else's pets,
and only in a dream did Penelope weep
for *her* slaughtered geese, their soft white strewn
round the water trough. When Telemachus strung
a wire between two trees and began hanging
the servant women, one by one, noosing
them in a line, the dying women
were described as thrushes spreading their wings,
doves or larks caught in a spring.
They were killed as a flock of birds, as undeserving
of the death of a single human being.
Though, first, in a colder, waking moment, the undisguised
Odysseus ordered the women to remove the corpses
from the great hall, to stack their lovers
in the yard. One cradling each beloved head,
another clutching at the feet,
the women became mere things—
their flesh a rag for scouring the furniture,
trying to scrub clear the appalling

table. Their last task
before being strangled—to dispose
of the earth itself, the blood-soaked floor
that Telemachus meticulously cut out,
so in the future—that narrow corridor
down which so many would be driven—a visitor
would not know she was invited into
a charnel house.

from *Partisan Review*

Postfeminism

◊　◊　◊

There are two kinds of people, soldiers and women,
as Virginia Woolf said. Both for decoration only.

Now that is too kind. It's technical: virgins and wolves.
We have choices now. Two little girls walk into a bar,

one orders a shirley temple. Shirley Temple's pimp
comes over and says you won't be sorry. She's a fine

piece of work but she don't come cheap. Myself, I'm
in less fear of predators than of walking around

in my mother's body. That's sneaky, that's more
than naked. Let's even it up: you go on fuming in your

gray room. I am voracious alone. Blank and loose,
metallic lingerie. And rare black-tipped cigarettes

in a handmade basket case. Which of us weaves
the world together with a quicker blue of armed

seduction: your war-on-thugs, my body stockings.
Ascetic or carnivore. Men will crack your glaze

even if you leave them before morning. Pigs
ride the sirens in packs. Ah, flesh, technoflesh,

there are two kinds of people. Hot with mixed
light, drunk with insult. You and me.

from *Chelsea*

from Black Series

◇   ◇   ◇

Then a dusk like this, a subversion of surfaces,
a vague expectancy of absence. Blurrings. Wings.
I watch the edges break and flee; they are Ophelias.

Soft town that settles on this land, town of inconclusiveness,
encryption, I touch your gateless air, your scaffoldless
upholdings. What covenants do you carry as you come,
what summonings provisioning your kingdom, and all the footless
crossings that move through you? What treaties and what pacts?
Blown leaves against the rotting fence, the jutting tilted heads
of rusted nails, they drift in a suspended radiance
that floods the skin like fear but isn't fear.

The yellow mullein stand tall against the house
as though they know they must negotiate this passage
as you conjure them away, your brain-darks reeling,
your glimmerings revising, interceding,
yet somehow they return by morning.

Now the sun's transit has gone under. The smallest splinterings
asleep it seems. Asleep the clear-lit custody of knowing.
Soft town, I am our citizen, though I am knot and barb
among your wanderings, and can feel the fraught circuitries
first calm then slash themselves in me, resisting,
the wanting-to-be-calmed extending itself to you
then pulling fiercely back, self-maiming,
and then the anxious glances rising, peering round,
and this grazing of fingertips like wind, these nervous fingertips
like wind—

doubt is a beautiful garment, if only I could wear it,
all silk and ashes, on my skin.

from *Seneca Review*

Semantics at Four P.M.

◇   ◇   ◇

He smiles, says *What's happening?*
and I say somewhere
someone's setting electrodes to someone's testicles
who's been immersed two hours in ice water

up to his shoulders, he can't remember
what day it used to be. Somewhere someone
is being disemboweled with a
serrated blade, fish-knife

to slit open two fresh trout
he had for dinner last
week, Wednesday celebration
sizzling in its battered aluminum pan

over an open campfire
in a clearing, gleaming
pan and fish and fire and the water
that put out the fire, and

he looks down at his intestines, small
and large uncoiling, spoiling
by the unpaved road, surprised
the slick should glisten so, even

at noon, this close
to the equator, is it still summer
there, I never can remember
seasons. Several things are

happening, someone is being kicked repeatedly
in the ribs by three cops (he's black, blue
by now too, purple boot
marks, bruise treads), someone else

keeps falling against the wet cement floor
of his holding cell, he can't stop
falling, somebody
stop him, then he does, stopped watch, old

-fashioned, with a broken
spring coil mechanism, and someone
could find it face-down on the sidewalk, hold it
up to the light, say *I can fix this,*

but doesn't. Somewhere four teenaged boys
are playing hackeysack by a stream bed
on the verge of story, one of them
has an erection he wants

to go down, and someone thinks about
dinner, someone says *Sure looks like rain.*

from *American Letters & Commentary*

RICHARD SIKEN

The Dislocated Room

◊ ◊ ◊

It was night for many miles and then the real stars in the purple sky,
   like little boats rowed out too far,
begin to disappear.
         And there, in the distance, not the promised land,
                                        but a Holiday Inn,
with bougainvillea growing through the chain link by the pool.
   The door swung wide: twin beds, twin lamps, twin plastic cups
wrapped up in cellophane
                  and he says *No Henry, let's not do this.*
Can you see the plot like dotted lines across the room?
   Here is the sink to wash away the blood,
here's the whiskey, the ripped-up shirt. Here is the tile of the bathroom
      floor, the disk of the drain
                  punched through with holes.
Here is the boy like a sack of meat, here are the engines, the little room
      that is not a room,
the Henry that is not a Henry, the Henry with a needle and thread,
      hovering over the hollow boy passed out
                        on the universal bedspread.
         Here he is again, being sewn up.
So now we have come to a great battlefield, the warmth of the fire,
      the fire still burning,
the heat escaping like a broken promise, the horizon widened
                           like an open road.
Henry's putting his hands all over him to keep him in the room,
      but the words keep rolling over the sleeper's lips:
                     He won't kiss me. He won't kiss me.
         But talking about God now, not boys.
This is the part where, this is the part where, this is the part where you

wake up in your clothes again,
this is the part where you're trying to stay inside the building.
        Stay in the room for now, he says. *Stay in the room*
                                    for now.
This is the place, you say to yourself, where everything
        starts to begin,
the wounds reveal a thicker skin and suddenly there is no floor.
                                Meanwhile,
there is something underneath the building that is trying very hard
                to get your attention.
Let's say you're dreaming about a devil with red skin and black horns,
        a man with almond eyes and a zipper that runs the length
of his spine.
        A standard devil.
                The one from the Underwood Ham label.
A man who is standing, cloven-hooved, in the middle of a Howard
        Johnson's, pointing at you with a glass of milk,
                saying *Drink this,*
                        before I break your bones.
You pinch yourself but you're still sleeping. You pinch yourself but
        you're still sleeping,
pinch yourself, you pinch yourself, you pinch . . .
                        but the man says take one, take it, here
is the first escape: pills, valves, a new velocity, and the voices
        are getting louder.
You can see the grill, the pots and pans, the apple pies
                        with their big sliced grins,
and you can see the shadow that the man is throwing across
        the linoleum,
how it resembles a boat, how it crosses the tiles just so,
                the masts of his arms rasping against the windows.
                                The bell rings, the dog growls,
and then the wind picking up, and the light falling, and his mouth
        flickering, and the dog
howling, and the window closing tight against the dirty rain.
                And he's pointing at you with a glass of milk
        as if he's trying to tell you that there is
some sort of shining star now buried deep inside you and he has to
                        dig it out with a knife.
Here is the hallway and here are the doors and here is the fear of the

162

other thing, the relentless
thing, your body drowning in gravity, but you are fighting it, and you
         want some help, and then the help arrives but
                                   it isn't helpful at all.
This is the meanwhile, the in-between, the waiting that happens in the
    space between
one note and the next, the part where you confuse
                          his hands with the room, the dog
    with the man, the blood with the ripped-up sky.
             Henry, he's saying. *Who is it that's talking?*
I thought I heard the clink
      of ice to teeth. I thought I heard the clink of teeth to glass.
                  The dog, his bowl, his sloppy grin,
the number of wounds, the exact sequence,
      the words now lurching in his mouth and drifting,
                    the words now drifting away.
He puts his hands, he's putting his hands, he puts his hands
                            all over you
to keep you in the room, but here is the Angel of Cornflakes and Milk,
    and here is the Angel of Open Wounds,
    and here is the Angel of Wash You Clean,
                the Angel of Taking It All Away.
We have not been given all the words necessary.
        We have not been given anything at all.
    We've been driving all night.
          We've been driving a long time.
We don't want to stop. We can't stop. He's standing over you.
                      His hands are open or
his hands are fists. It's night. It's noon. He's driving. It's happening
    all over again.
      It isn't happening. It's love or it isn't. It isn't over.
You're in a car. You're in the weeds again. You're on a bumpy road
      and there are criminals everywhere,
                   longing for danger.
Open the door and the light falls in. Open your mouth and it falls
    right out again.
He's on top of you. He's next to you, right next to you in fact.
      He has the softest skin wrapped entirely around him.
                      It isn't him.
It isn't you. You're falling now. You're swimming. This is not

harmless. You are not
  breathing. You're climbing out of the chlorinated pool again.
Is there an acceptable result? Do we mean something when we talk?
  Is it enough that we are shuddering
           from the sound?
Left hand raising the fork to the mouth, feeling the meat slide down
  your throat, thinking
     My throat. Mine. Everything in this cone of light is mine.
The ashtray and the broken lamp, the filthy orange curtains and his
  ruined shirt.
       I've been in your body, baby, and it was paradise.
 I've been in your body and it was a carnival ride.
You're inside you. He's inside you. He's between the two of you.
   You're the residue.
      Gold bodies in a red red room.
You are here. You are not here. You're the room. You're in the room.
  You aren't in the room.
     Stay here for just a little longer.
They want to stop but they can't stop. They don't know what
             they're doing.
This is not harmless, the *how to touch it,* we do not want the screen
  completely
lifted from our eyes, just lifted long enough to see the holes.
   Tired and sore and rubbed the wrong way,
      rubbed raw and throbbing in the light.
They want to stop but they don't stop. They cannot get the bullet out.
   Cut me open and the light streams out.
 Stitch me up and the light keeps streaming out between
         the stitches.
He cannot get the bullet out, he thinks, he can't, and then, he does.
  A little piece of grit to build a pearl around.
Midnight June. Midnight July. They've been going at it for days now.
  Getting the bullet out.
Digging out the bullet and holding it up to the light, the light.
    Digging out the bullet and holding it up to the light.

    from *Indiana Review*

Mother of Us All

◇　◇　◇

Mother of the long silences
that pinned us to our chairs,
where were you in your body
if not here with us?

Mother of the stolen roses
that faded like kisses,
why so pale by the window,
peering in at us?

Mother of the prayer beads
that pooled on our pillows,
what were you murmuring,
hands like paper pressed from us?

Mother of the snakes
that coiled around each wrist,
did it ever occur to you to poison us?

Mother of the mirrors
that disassembled the walls,
how many times did we see you look beyond us?

Mother of the incessant purges
that sent our beautiful books and toys to charity,
what perfect world had you not already given us?

Mother of the busy hands
that tore at the spiked tongues,
what were you pulling, hiding at dusk from us?

Mother of the white hair
that sprouted overnight,
what made you skittish,
lock every door behind us?

Mother of the diminishing voice
that broke into chalk,
how could we have known there were things
you had wanted to tell us?

Mother of the disappearance
that shadowed Father's face,
when did you decide you had to leave us.

from *Shenandoah* and *Poetry Daily*

Chit-Chat with
the Junior League Women

◇   ◇   ◇

A Junior League woman in blue
Showed me enough panty
To keep my back straight,
To keep my wine glass lifting
Every three minutes,
Time enough for the sun to wrench
More sweat from the workers
Shouldering cement and lumber,
The scaffolding of hard labor
That keeps this hill view up.
Do you have children? she asked.
Oh, yes, I chimed. Sip, sip.
Her legs spread just enough to stir
The lint from my eyelashes,
Just enough to think of a porpoise
Smacking me with sea-scented kisses.
The Junior League woman in yellow
Turned to the writer next to me,
Bearded fellow with two remaindered books,
His words smoldering for any goddamn reader.
This gave me time. Sip, sip,
Then a hard, undeceitful swallow
Of really good Napa Valley wine.
My mind, stung with drink,
Felt tight, like it had panty hose
Over its cranium. I thought

About the sun between sips,
How I once told my older brother,
Pale vampire of psychedelic music,
That I was working on a tan.
That summer my mom thought I had worms—
I was thin as a flattened straw,
Nearly invisible, a mere vapor
As I biked up and down the block.
I rolled out an orange towel in the back yard
And sun sucked more weight
From my body. After two hours,
My skin hollered. . . . I let the reminiscence
Pass and reached for the bottle,
Delicately because I was in a house
With a hill view held up by cement and lumber
And other people's work.
A Junior League woman in red
Sat with her charming hands
On her lap, studying us two writers,
Now with the panty hose of drunkenness
Pulled over our heads and down to our eyes.
What do you do exactly, Mr. Soto?
And I looked at her blinding
Underwear and—sip, sip—said, Everything.

from *Poetry*

In a Field
Outside the Town

◇ ◇ ◇

Three days later, Suljic was finally given a drink
of water and marched with a dozen other men
onto a small livery truck, one of two, fenced
along each side by wooden planks,

the back left open to give a clear shot
to the automatic weapon poking out the window
of the red sedan that followed, the squat nose
trained on them, ridiculously, as if they'd any thought

of hopping off a moving truck. Suljic peered
vacantly through the slats. He'd missed the yellow flowers
of Spring and by now saw a landscape taken over
by Summer, the grasses closing behind them as they veered

from the road and lurched across cow paths. They drove
to the center of a wide field and stopped. Old sweat,
without the breeze of movement, prickled in the heat.
A metal smell drifted, an untended apple grove

baked on a hill, and the weeds droned, motory with bees.
But Suljic noticed none of these, fixed instead
on the gaps in the field where bodies, all dead,
matted down the wild carrot and chicory, their khakis

splotched darkly, like a fawn's dappled haunches
obscuring them. The men clambered down into the tall grass

and lined up at gunpoint. Suljic was sure the last
good thing he'd ever see would be the apple branches

drooping with fruit, but the men beside him grabbed
his hand, and looked him in the face, as if
Suljic, just a bricklayer, had any assurances to give.
He squeezed the hand back, hard, and felt a scab

crossing the man's knuckles. He saw, too, a thin scar
worrying the arch of his left eyebrow, much older,
perhaps from a fall as a child from a ladder
picking fruit. His hand was like a clump of mortar,

and three nights without sleep had webbed his eyes red.
And Suljic suddenly stuttered to ask his name,
what town was he from, his job—anything—but there came
the crackle, like sometimes thunder, undecided

whether to begin, that starts, stalls, then trips
over itself, the sound crinkling from one
end of the sky to the other. The sound took possession
of his face until it, too, crinkled, his grip

pulsed, and he fell forward. Suljic winced
in the tackle of bodies, and splayed down in the dirt
flattening himself like a beetle, not hurt
in any new way, not yet convinced

he wasn't dead and didn't feel it. He heard the click
of fresh clips sliding into place, and shut
his eyes lightly, sure someone had seen he wasn't shot
and would come finish it. But no one came. Another truck

rolled up. The men climbed down, and lined up, docilely.
He recognized, solely by rhythm, a prayer, cut off
by the crackle, the hush of crickets, the soft
whump of bodies folding at the knees

and knocked by bullets shoulder first
into the grass. No one yelled. No one tried to run.

Another truck, another group, falling like a succession
of bricks sliding off a hod. Suljic finally pissed

where he lay, and blended in all the better
with the others. The noise stopped, and he cracked
his eyes enough to see, across the backs
like bleeding hills, a man strolling along the scatter

of bodies with a pistol, putting a slug
into the skull of anyone that still twitched
or mumbled. Then came the snort and low-pitched
rumble of diesel engines as two backhoes dug

a trench along the margin of all the collapsed
bodies. Impossibly, the crackling started anew,
and when darkness finally settled, the squads continued
in what light the backhoes' headlights threw. Perhaps

the shooting was over long before the sound
left him, the crackle to his eardrums
was like the rolling of a boat to his limbs
echoing long after he'd reached dry ground.

The soldiers left. Still he didn't move, but eased
his eyes full open. The moon above the orchard
was shrinking higher, its light glossing the awkward
pale forms that stubbled the dry weeds,

glinting off teeth and eyes. He scuttled from beneath
the arms and legs flopped sleepingly over
his own, as though by drunkards or lovers,
and rose like a foal to his numb feet,

seeing throughout the field no man not touched
by three dead others. He stood for a moment, trying
to guess, even roughly, their number multiplying
bodies per square yard, but the math was too much,

the count too huge. He stared at the faces beside him
in the grass, like a man leaving something he knew

he would someday have to return to,
looking for the landmarks that would guide him—

the crooked teeth, the welted cheek, the pale eyes eclipsed
by half-shut lids, lolling upward, inward, swollen
as though with weeping, blood from an unseen hole
glistering down a chin line, crusting on lips.

How could he explain his life, what could he say
to those who weren't here to see, to the mothers and wives
who'd swear for years their men were still alive,
somewhere, the bodies never found, bulldozed into clay—

would he tell them how he tiptoed, unable to avoid
stepping on hands and ankles, or how the tears
like a secret he'd harbored through three years
of siege shook loose, and how he let them, no longer afraid

of being found out and cut down by gunfire,
or how he ran anyway, when he reached the open, quick
as his bum leg would let him, without a look
back at the faces turned like gourds in the dark mire.

from *Poetry*

172

A . E . S T A L L I N G S

Asphodel

◇ ◇ ◇

(after the words of Penny Turner, Nymphaion, Greece)

Our guide turned in her saddle, broke the spell:
"You ride now through a field of asphodel,
The flower that grows on the plains of hell.

Across just such a field the pale shade came
Of proud Achilles, who had preferred a name
And short life to a long life without fame,

And summoned by Odysseus he gave
This wisdom, 'Better by far to be a slave
Among the living, than great among the grave.'

I used to wonder, how did such a bloom
Become associated with the tomb?
Then one evening, walking through the gloom,

I noticed a strange fragrance. It was sweet,
Like honey—but with hints of rotting meat.
An army of them bristled at my feet."

from *Beloit Poetry Journal*

Wings

◇　◇　◇

If you could have wings would you want them?

　　I don't know.

I mean, if you could use them to fly, would you want them?

　　Yes, if I could fly.

But they would be really big.

　　How big?

They might brush against your knees as you walked, or be bigger than
some doorways.
　　And what if you couldn't ever take them off?

　　I still would want them.

If you couldn't take them off, even if you were going somewhere,
　　or going to bed, or eating at a table, or you wanted to pick
　　someone up, you could never take them off?

　　Yes, I would. I would still want them.

Because you could fly?

　　Yes, because of the flying.

And if they were heavy, or even if no one else had them, and even if
   your children and their children didn't have them?

Yes, I think so.

But you would still have arms and hands and legs, and you could still
   speak, but you had wings, too. You would want the wings, too?

Yes, I would want the wings, too.

And when you were walking around, people would stare at you, and they
   wouldn't necessarily understand that you could fly?

I understand. I understand that they wouldn't understand.

Or if people thought they meant something, something they didn't really
   mean?

I would know what the wings were for.

And if you had them, forever—the forever, I mean, that is your life,
   you would still want them?

Yes, I would want them. I would take them, so long as I could fly

that I might fly away

   that I might fly away where the ships

      *that I might fly away where the ships of pine wood pass
      between the dark cliffs.*

from *The American Poetry Review*

The English Canon

◇   ◇   ◇

It's not that the first speakers left out women
Unless they were goddesses, harlots, or impossible loves
Seen from afar, often while bathing,

And it's not that the only parts my grandfathers could have played
Were as extras in Xanadu,
Nor that it gives no instructions for shopping or cooking.

The trouble is, I've spent my life
Getting over the lyrics
That taught me to brush my hair till it's gleaming,

Stay slim, dress tastefully, and not speak of sex,
Death, violence, or the desire for any of them,
And to let men do the talking and warring

And bringing of the news. I know a girl's got to protest
These days, but she also has to make money
And do her share of journalism and combat,

And she has to know from the gut whom to trust,
Because what do her teachers know, living in books,
And what does she know, starting from scratch?

from *New Letters*

PAMELA SUTTON

There Is a Lake of Ice
on the Moon

◊　◊　◊

Inna Cherniahivsky must be dead by now. I promised
to visit, but I never did. One time I started
up the steps of the Philadelphia row home—
my first East Coast home—but faltered
at a puddle where the marble step had been worn
by habit, years, and rain.
There is a lake of ice on the moon. Life,
on other planets, is possible now, they say.
Once I almost rented a ruined apartment
with a balcony overlooking the most exquisite
trees—bark, purple-brown, just after the rain.
An expensive therapist told me I could see
only the trees. This was the problem.
I had no judgment or the wrong kind.
I had been raised in the country but lived
in the city. The problem, he said, I was from
the Midwest—the upper Midwest. It was true:
Each winter I hiked through knee-deep snow
to the lake—skates flung over my shoulder.
There was a chill while switching footwear,
but then so much pleasure lacing the skates
to the perfect tension. And for a few hours
each day, each winter, between gelid discs of fire
and ice, that lake was mine. And the intimate
trees posed just for me. And places too far, too
deep to swim in summer, I could skate over—

blades cutting the surface. I could leap and land
hard—hearing, seeing, the ice boom and crack.
It never broke. Life was possible. Judgment,
perfect then; useless now. Who needs to know
in Philadelphia, the myriad colors of frozen water,
the wind chill factor, the angle of the sun, to judge
the thickness and quality of ice? And the trees—
could my therapist distinguish the eyes of a wolf
from knots in pine? Does he know the meaning of North—
sun setting at midnight—the uselessness
of clocks—seduction of hypothermia—or why one small
puddle on a marble stair can stop me cold?
When I was too young for the lake my father
made a pool of ice for me in the yard by running
the garden hose. He gave me double-bladed skates
for steadiness. It was night. It was bitter. But stars
like birches splintered the black forest sky.
Inna Cherniahivsky must be dead by now.
There is a lake of ice on the moon.

from *The American Poetry Review*

No Palms

◇　◇　◇

No palms dolled up the tedium, no breathing wind.
No problem was the buzzword then, their way to go.

In truth, my case was black as sin, a thing to hide,
In that they feigned to find me sane, so not to know.

Someone brought in a medium. Anathema!
Some clown sewed up my eyes, he said it wouldn't show.

Confusing hands with craze, they howled, "Let's cut them off."
Confusing, too, their spies, my lies without an echo.

Time and again they stitched my mind with warp and woof.
Time pounded in my ruby heart, doing a slow,

Slow dim-out in that lupanar, slow take, slow fade,
Slow yawning like a door. "Hello," I said. "HELLO."

There, flung across the room between inside and out,
There must have shown itself to me . . . an afterglow.

With such a blaze to celebrate where centuries meet
With time itself, how could I hesitate? Although

Still trapped in the millennium I knew I had
Still time to blow some kisses. Look up, there they go!

from *The Yale Review*

Limen

◇   ◇   ◇

All day I've listened to the industry
of a single woodpecker, worrying the catalpa tree
just outside my window. Hard at his task,

his body is a hinge, a door knocker
to the cluttered house of memory in which
I can almost see my mother's face.

She is there, again, beyond the tree,
its slender pods and heart-shaped leaves,
hanging wet sheets on the line—each one

a thin white screen between us. So insistent
is this woodpecker, I'm sure he must be
looking for something else—not simply

the beetles and grubs inside, but some other gift
the tree might hold. All day he's been at work,
tireless, making the green hearts flutter.

from *New England Review*

Song

◊   ◊   ◊

words & sounds that build bridges toward a new tongue
within the vortex of cadences, magic weaves there
a mystery, syncopating music rising from breath of the young,

the syllables spraying forward like some cloud or mist hung
around the day, evening, under streetlamps, yeasting air, where
words & sounds that build bridges toward a new tongue

gather, lace the language like fireflies stitching the night's lungs,
rhythms of new speech reinventing themselves with a flair,
a mystery, syncopating music, rising from breath of the young,

where the need for invention at the tongue's edge, high-strung,
at the edge of the cliff, becomes a risk-taking poet who shares
words & sounds that build bridges toward a new tongue,

full of wind & sun, breath feeds poetry from art's aqualungs,
under a blue sea that is sky, language threads itself through air
a mystery, syncopating music, rising from breath of the young,

is a solo snatched from the throat of pure utterance, sung,
or wordsmiths blues-ing cadences, weaving lines into prayers,
words & sounds that build bridges toward a new tongue—
a mystery, syncopating music, rising from breath of the young

from *Tin House*

Rahim Multani

◇ ◇ ◇

How can a woman resolve
her marriage, save by lies? I have not learned
from others. I speak of my own life. She
stays at home, the man goes forth. A husband's
absence, a daughter's
anger, a lover's
suspicion—that is her lot.
—RICHARD HOWARD (from "1915")

I. KING PRAWNS

When Kiran went out of town I took the girls to get haircuts in Delhi.
It wasn't often I could get there. But I wasn't the youngest bride any-
more, and I could be seen out with Kiran's friends.

Hard liquor, parties, everyone had been to London, Hong Kong, New
York; you could smell the foreign currency in the smiles—cold pepper-
mint, white nickel, then the warm gold around our necks like foil.
She's a beauty. She I envy. He's minting money. He's a prince and
always will be. And how is Lokhun? Long time we have not seen
Amrita. That's the way it went at night, sip, sip, we smiled between the
facts we traded, the lies we harbored, or the truths we harbored and the
lies we spread like cheer. Who's earning what and who we would slan-
der was our game. We all had money, drivers, got haircuts at Con-
naught, bought Swiss chocolates, and these were nights we wore our
best saris, women everywhere rustling in the room.

II. A DROPPED SHAWL

There he was, Rahim, owner of the Delhi Palace Grand, in raw silk,
Nehru jacket and trousers; Kiran's cousin, not a cousin, but a neighbor
in the Bombay refugee camp. He'd made his family's money again. He
had backers; and he charmed me with a headwaiter's fastidious air. He
told me things about Kiran I never knew, courage during the Hindu-
Muslim protests of the forties. And British Quit India. Kiran would
fight, hell with Gandhi's salt march.

Then Rahim told me to stop by the Delhi Grand. I should come by
myself and stay a week if I could.

From the back of a bookshelf he got a flask of scotch. I wore a wool
blouse and shawl. The main room buzzed with chatter. Rahim pressed
closer. *Remove your shawl, the room is heated.* It was and so I did. I felt like
the beach at Malpai clear of the broad palms, a stretch of sand to sweep
your eyes over. Then I knew everything. A dropped shawl led to a
dropped jacket, his breath the heat of a hand; it is just what I wanted,
Rahim in any room. Kiran, he was on a plane over London. Rahim was
his cousin, not his cousin; but a brother from the camp, not a brother;
his best friend.

III. IF ONLY A TASTE

A car came from the Delhi Grand
I packed my bag and took the train home
His voice trailed   drop your bag and come to me
What he wanted I wanted
Me all my life I said yes because you wanted me to
but this time I meant it

Did I mean it? I did
Would I again? I would
I think of the hotel
the cool stroke he left on my shoulder after he took off my shawl
He poured me a scotch
His look asked would you and I said I would

IV. A HUSBAND'S RETURN

I was expecting rain for a week no rain came
Like a heavy period waiting for the blood to drop
Kiran his car pulled in I found myself
wearing a smile I could not fathom Rahim
he quickly burnt away like morning
mist a stick of wheat blown off a—

a catch in the mouth Kiran kissed
me absently a landlord on his land
a warrior with no rivals
I felt dutiful and guilty sealed and
unconcealed my skin
held Rahim's scent and nothing else

from *Meridian*

PAUL VIOLI

As I Was Telling David and Alexandra Kelley

◇   ◇   ◇

My brother swears this is true.
And others have willingly,
—generously testified,
as they did that other time when
after leaving an office party
they pulled off the expressway,
walked into a place he'd never
been to before, and ordered
a few more drinks while he
headed for the lavatory.
But as he was crossing the dining room
on the other side of the bar
this vicious fight broke out.
Two women—well-dressed, tall,
gorgeous—tore into each other,
punching, clawing, swinging
spike-heeled shoes, pulling
each other's hair, and my brother,
aghast, jumped between them
to break it up, grabbed them roughly,
held them apart, berated
them, tried to shake some sense
into—when he gradually pieced
it all together: the changed look
on their faces, the disapproval,
the utter silence of condemnation

that everyone aimed not at the
women, but at him, the fact that
it was a supper club theatre
and he had just jumped into
the climactic scene of a play—
But this, I hasten to add, is not
about my brother but his neighbor,
a man whose roof needed repair;
a man who, more than most, feared heights.
A ladder, to this neighbor,
didn't ordinarily suggest the kind
of elevating work that joins
the material to the spiritual,
so before mounting it he called
his children over and, as he wrapped
a rope thick enough to moor a barge
around his waist and lashed
the other end around the car bumper,
carefully explained to them
how they should steady the ladder
until he had climbed onto the roof.
Up he went, not overstepping
but securing both feet on the same rung
before proceeding to the next:
a trembling man on a trembling ladder.
He squirmed over the drain,
crawled up the not very steep slope,
flopped over the peak, then slid
inch by inch down the rear slope
until he felt confident enough
to kneel instead of crawl,
to sigh and take a deep breath
before he began to cut a shingle.
Perhaps the first horripilating signal
was a subtle tug on the rope,
like an angel plucking a harp string.
Perhaps it was a sudden tautness
around his waist, or, perhaps,
he heard the station wagon door
slam shut, then the ignition,

the engine roar to life, or
slowly grindingly churn before it
kicked in and he was yanked heavenward
then jerked back, slammed, twisted,
keel-hauled belly up, belly down,
over the roof, dashed onto the
driveway to be dragged, dribbled,
bounced along the road, his
wife looking this way and that
as she drove on, wondering
wherever were those screams coming from?
Doctors, police, all believed
she could very well have not seen
the rope; could not, with windows
rolled up, have ascertained,
while they lasted, the source,
proximity, and intensity of the screams.
And I, for one, though respectful of
the family's desire for privacy,
think for numerous, inevitable,
irresistible philosophical,
sociological but mostly religious
reasons, this place, this event,
this man deserves a shrine
which, if donations are forthcoming
I am willing to oversee
the construction of
at 145 Sampson Avenue,
Islip, Long Island, New York.
That's right, that's the name
of the place: Islip. I swear.

from *The World*

Pissarro at Dusk

◇　◇　◇

I.

I suppose I should have told you about Louveciennes
and the other villages where he took a house

with his brood of seven, shown where this street ends
and that lane forks, those walks of a Pontoise

I have never seen except as his accompanying
shadow on leaf glued autumn pavements, or

crunching bright piebald snow, but I kept seeing
things through his eyes: a gate, a rusted door,

since all our radiant bush, a road, a hill
with torches of pouis, a shade-stayed stream

made joy recede to memory, our provincial
palms, bowing, withdraw before his dream,

as History's distance shrank a crescent fringe
of rustling yellow fronds on a white shore,

a house, a harbor with its mountain range
to a dot named by its cartographer

the name longer than the dot. In Trinidad,
there was one painter, the Frenchman Cazabon

whose embalmed *paysages* were all we had,
our mongrel culture gnawing its one bone.

Cazabon and Pissarro; the first is ours,
the second found the prism that was Paris,

rooted in France, his dark-soiled ancestors;
no matter, cherish the conviction their work carries.

II.

Affliction: inflammation of the eyes
that often stops him painting. The tears run,

but older than tears is the paralysis
of doubt, unchanged from when he first began,

since man is a small island who contains
cisterns of sorrow, and drought that absence dries,

and doubt; St. Thomas hazing as it rains
and love, the mist-bow bent on paradise.

In his life's dusk, though hand and eye grow weary,
his concentration strengthens in its skill

some critics think his work is ordinary,
but the ordinary is the miracle.

Ordinary love and ordinary death,
ordinary suffering, ordinary birth,

the ordinary couplets of our breath,
ordinary heaven, ordinary earth.

To watch the moving sea, heavy and silver
on a mid-August afternoon, then turn

his catalogue of views of the great river
dragging its barges, so little time to learn,

you are taken there, though, by his brush's
delicate frenzy, by all his tenderness

even for winter scenes when the snow hushes
the rasping surface and a boulevard's noise.

My Paris comes out of his canvases
not from a map, and perhaps, even better

than Paris itself; they fill these verses
with their own light, their walks, their weather

that will outlast me as they outlast him,
their hustling crowds, their carriages in strokes

fresh, fast and trembling, as in a film
where wheels stop and run backwards, silver spokes

of drizzle down this boulevard, that park
where I can gaze at leisure, taking time

to loiter at each stroke, at the faint arc
of a white bridge; so modest, so sublime!

III.

Paint a true street in Anse La Raye, Choiseul,
the roasting asphalt, the bleached galvanize roofs

grooved like these lines, paint the dark heat as well
inside the canted shacks, do the blurred hooves

of a boy whooping a white mare near a lagoon
for gone Gauguin, paint the violet bruise

of reef under watery wiry at noon
paint the Cathedral's solace, the canoes

resting in the almonds, always the same
canoes resting under the almonds, and next you could

paint the thick flowers too poor to have a name,
that couple entering a shading wood

for something no longer your business,
mix the light's color with that pliant knife

that is your plasterer's trowel. It would be nice
to do this in deep gratitude for your life,

just as its hallelujahs praise their giver
the chalk white chapel portals of La Fargue

before L'aouvière Dorée the sun-gilt river
whose missal shallows recite your epilogue.

IV.

Our tribes were shaken like seeds from a sieve.
Our dialects, rooted, forced their own utterance,

and what were we without the slow belief
in our own nature? Not Guinea, not Provence.

And yet so many fled, so many lost
to the magnetic spires of cities, not the cedars,

as if a black pup turned into the ghost
of the white hound, but a search that will lead us

where we began; to islands, not the busy
but unchanged patronage of the empire's center,

guests at the roaring feast of Veronese,
or Tiepolo's Moors, where once we could not enter.

Camille Pissarro must have heard the noise
of loss-lamenting slaves, and if he did,

they tremble in the poplars of Pontoise,
the trembling, elegiac tongues he painted.

Swivel the easel down, drill it in sand,
then tighten the canvas against vaps of wind,

straddle the stool, reach for the brush with one hand
then pour the oil in trembling sacrament.

There is another book that is the shadow
of my hand on this sunlit page, the one

I have tried hard to write, but let this do;
let gratitude redeem what lies undone.

from *The New Republic*

Fabrications

◊　◊　◊

As if to prove again
The bright resilience of the frailest form,
A spider has repaired her broken web
Between the palm-trunk and the jasmine tree.

Etched on the clear new light
Above the still-imponderable ground,
It is a single and gigantic eye
Whose golden pupil, now, the spider is.

Through it you catch the flash
Of steeples brightened as a cloud slips over,
One loitering star, and off there to the south
Slow vultures kettling in the lofts of air.

Each day men frame and weave
In their own way whatever looms in sight,
Though they must see with human scale and bias,
And though there is much unseen. The Talmud tells

How dusty travelers once
Came to a river where a roe was wading,
And would have hastened then to strip and bathe,
Had not a booming voice from heaven said,

"Step not into that water:
Seven years since, a joiner dropped his axe
Therein, and it hath not yet reached the bottom."
Whether beneath our senses or beyond them,

The world is bottomless,
A drift of star-specks or the Red King's dream,
And fogs our thought, although it is not true
That we grasp nothing till we grasp it all.

Witness this ancient map
Where so much blank and namelessness surround
A little mushroom-clump of coastal towers
In which we may infer civility,

A harbor-full of spray,
And all those loves which hint of love itself,
Imagining too a pillar at whose top
A spider's web upholds the architrave.

from *The Yale Review*

SUSAN WOOD

Analysis of the Rose
As Sentimental Despair

◇ ◇ ◇

Cy Twombley, set of five paintings, 1985

for Larry Levis (1946–1996)

Here it is, the Impressionist garden
raised to another level of fluidity,
like late Monet, no shape assembling
itself in a wash of pink and red,

a watery garden where one color flows
into another, roses blazing and bleeding,
pink, crimson, carmine, scarlet,
until the color flames to blood,

the colors from his own heart,
and the heart, too, blazes and breaks
open, beauty giving way
to death, the eternal

in the ephemeral. No, not giving way
exactly, it's embedded in the bud, the vein.
Rose, oh sheer contradiction—
what made the poets weep whose words fly

like flags above the paintings.
Those early-waking grievers—Rumi,
Rilke, Leopardi—oh, how each of them loved his sadness.
. . . his pains are delectable, his flames are like water.

They were bereft without their pain.
And I am thinking now
of the women they could never quite love
(loving the Idea, but not the Thing itself),

loving the memory of rose petals
strewn across a bed, but not
the rumpled, semen-stained sheets.
I am thinking of Clara Westhoff

to Paula Becker: "I am so very housebound. . . .
a house that has to be built—and built
and built—and the whole world
stands there around me. And it will not let me go."

And I am also thinking
of my friend Larry Levis, a poet
who loved Rilke, who wrapped himself
in his despair, the way he might have

worn an old quilt all through
one Thanksgiving in Iowa City
when the heat didn't work. It would have
warmed and comforted him. That was long ago,

before betrayal, divorce, all the old
home remedies for pain—Marcia and Larry
were still together then, and I remember
envying them that. I don't remember

what we ate or what we talked about,
all three of us poets—poetry, probably,
instead of love—but I remember
the black lakes of his eyes, the eyes

of an old man even then,
though he was my age, not even forty,
the way he touched his mustache
and laughed ruefully at his own bad jokes.

I don't know what had wounded him.
About grief he was "enthusiastic, but wrong,"
as he said of his students' poems.
When we laughed, our breath

drew clouds in the air
above the rented dining room table.
But here, in these paintings, the clouds
are roses, clouds of them drifting

and spilling over in the rain, a lake
of roses, roses streaked with rain,
so many of them you can't tell
one from another. If to know beauty is to live

with loss, then why should we love
our grief so much? It's nothing special.
And if death is the extinguishing of all form,
as the painter sees, it is also the rose made new

again and again, as he also sees,
the way I once stood, lost
in my sorrow, in the shallows
of Deer Lake. Above me, the live oaks

reached out their arms the way a mother
might open her arms for her child
to step inside, and Cosmo barked and ran
back and forth across the narrow dam,

until he slipped and fell and came up
swimming. He had a look of such surprise
that he could stay afloat! And then
I raised my face to the place where the sun

stole through the dense heaven of leaves,
and for a moment—just one, though it was enough—
I was somewhere else, I was a body
composed almost wholly of light.

And Larry? Years later, he died.
His heart just blazed and burst
open. It was spring, maybe roses bloomed
beside the back steps of his house in Virginia.

It was days before anyone found him, his face
already beginning to disappear, like a drawing
slowly being erased around the edges.
Most of the time he'd been troubled,

I don't know why exactly—the lovelorn
vineyards of California? the poverty
of horses?—for no reason and many reasons,
maybe, and maybe just because he was himself,

a man who courted his despair, shyly,
tenderly, the way he courted women,
but he was sober, writing again,
and after he died his friend took the poems

and made a book of elegies, as all poems are,
a book I am holding right now. Once,
when he was young, he wrote a poem
set on the morning after his death.

My body is a white thing . . . now,
he wrote. . . . *And there is nothing left but these flies,*
polished and swarming frankly in the sun.

What did his sorrow ever do for him?
It couldn't save him, anymore than love could.
But that's not the point. What *is* the point?
To know death, to breathe deeply

of its aroma, to hold it close to the heart
as one might hold a rose, and still desire
to go on living, that is the human,
the remarkable thing. For a long time, he did.

Now he is water, rose petals
in an Impressionist garden, these rose petals
dashed to the ground, drifting and blowing
in the late spring rain.

from *Ploughshares*

Borrowed Love Poems

◇ ◇ ◇

1)

What can I do, I have dreamed of you so much
What can I do, lost as I am in the sky

What can I do, now that all
the doors and windows are open

I will whisper this in your ear
as if it were a rough draft

something I scribbled on a napkin
I have dreamed of you so much

there is no time left to write
no time left on the sundial

for my shadow to fall back to the earth
lost as I am in the sky

2)

What can I do, all the years that we talked
and I was afraid to want more

What can I do, now that these hours
belong to neither you nor me

Lost as I am in the sky
What can I do, now that I cannot find

the words I need
when your hair is mine

now that there is no time to sleep
now that your name is not enough

3)

What can I do, if a red meteor wakes the earth
and the color of robbery is in the air

Now that I dream of you so much
my lips are like clouds

drifting above the shadow of one who is asleep
Now that the moon is enthralled with a wall

What can I do, if one of us is lying on the earth
and the other is lost in the sky

4)

What can I do, lost as I am in the wind
and lightning that surrounds you

What can I do, now that my tears
are rising toward the sky

only to fall back
into the sea again

What can I do, now that this page is wet
now that this pen is empty

5)

What can I do, now that the sky
has shut its iron door

and bolted clouds
to the back of the moon

now that the wind
has diverted the ocean's attention

now that a red meteor
has plunged into the lake

now that I am awake
now that you have closed the book

6)

Now that the sky is green
and the air is red with rain

I never stood in
the shadow of pyramids

I never walked from village to village
in search of fragments

that had fallen to earth in another age
What can I do, now that we have collided

on a cloudless night
and sparks rise

from the bottom of a thousand lakes

7)

To some, the winter sky is a blue peach
teeming with worms

and the clouds are growing thick
with sour milk

What can I do, now that the fat black sea
is seething

now that I have refused to return
my borrowed dust to the butterflies

their wings full of yellow flour

8)

What can I do, I never believed happiness
could be premeditated

What can I do, having argued with the obedient world
that language will infiltrate its walls

What can I do, now that I have sent you
a necklace of dead dried bees

and now that I want to
be like the necklace

and turn flowers into red candles
pouring from the sun

9)

What can I do, now that I have spent my life
studying the physics of good-bye

every velocity and particle in all the waves
undulating through the relapse of a moment's fission

now that I must surrender this violin
to the sea's foaming black tongue

now that January is almost here
and I have started celebrating a completely different life

10)

Now that the seven wonders of the night
have been stolen by history

Now that the sky is lost and the stars
have slipped into a book

Now that the moon is boiling
like the blood where it swims

Now that there are no blossoms left
to glue to the sky

What can I do,
I who never invented anything

and who dreamed of you so much
I was amazed to discover

the claw marks of those
who preceded us across this burning floor

from *Boston Review*

The Infirmament

◊ ◊ ◊

An end is always punishment for a beginning.
If you're Catholic, sadness is punishment
for happiness, you become the bug you squash
if you're Hindu, a flinty space opens
in your head after a long night of laughter
and wine. For waking there are dreams,
for French poetry, English poetry,
for light, fire although sometimes
fire must be punished by light
which is why psychotherapy had to be invented.
A father may say nothing to a son for years.
A wife may keep something small folded deep
in her underwear drawer. Clouds come in
resembling the terrible things we believe
about ourselves, a rock comes loose
from a ledge, the baby cries
and cries. Doll in a chair,
windshield wipers, staring off
into the city lights. For years
you may be unable to hear the word *monkey*
without a stab in the heart because
she called you that the summer she thought
she loved you and you thought you loved
someone else and everyone loved
your salad dressing. And the daffodils
come up in the spring and the snow covers
the road in winter and the water covers
the deep trenches in the sea where all the time

the inner stuff of this earth surges up
which is how the continents are made
and broken.

from *New American Writing*

CONTRIBUTORS'
NOTES AND
COMMENTS

KIM ADDONIZIO was born in Washington, D.C., in 1954. She currently teaches workshops in the San Francisco Bay Area. Her collections of poetry are *The Philosopher's Club* (1994), *Jimmy & Rita* (1997), and *Tell Me* (2000), all from BOA Editions. With Dorianne Laux, she is coauthor of *The Poet's Companion: A Guide to the Pleasures of Writing Poetry* (Norton, 1997). A book of stories, *In the Box Called Pleasure* (1999), was published by Fiction Collective 2.

Addonizio writes: "I had never seen Ingmar Bergman's 'Virgin Spring,' and when it turned up on TV late one night while I was flipping channels, I settled in to watch it. I felt, frankly, that it would be good for me, and that I ought to watch it, more than I expected to enjoy it or to be moved. I had vague memories of seeing some of Bergman's films when I was around nineteen, and thinking they were tedious and depressing. But now I found myself mesmerized. I'm obsessed with evil, probably due in part to my Catholic upbringing, and writing about the film was another way to ask the questions I always ask: Where do we locate justice, good and evil, innocence and guilt? I don't think the film supplies any answers, and of course the poem doesn't, either. If I knew the answers I don't think the poem would be very interesting; I tend not to like poems, or poets, who resolve the difficult questions of life with some epiphanic moment of transcendence. And when I do it myself, I wish I'd been able to dig a little deeper."

PAMELA ALEXANDER was born in Natick, Massachusetts, in 1948, and earned an MFA from the University of Iowa after graduating from Bates College. She worked at various jobs (newspaper reporter, secretary, emergency medical technician) until James Merrill chose her first book, *Navigable Waterways* (Yale, 1985), for the Yale Younger Poet Award. She taught poetry writing at the Massachusetts Institute of Technology for thirteen years, and began teaching and codirecting the creative writing program at Oberlin College in 1997. *Commonwealth of Wings,* a sequence of poems based on the life of John James Audubon, was published by Wesleyan in 1991; her third book, *Inland,* won the Iowa Prize in 1997 and was published by the University of Iowa Press. She has received fellowships from the Bunting Institute of Radcliffe College and from the Fine Arts Work Center in Provincetown, Massachusetts.

Alexander writes: "Most poems are work—making them is pleasurable, but labor-intensive. Occasionally, however, a poem assembles itself. 'Semiotics' did so, quickly and economically, with whatever was at hand. My violist neighbor (of the St. Petersburg Quartet) practiced so much and so hauntingly that I had a chronic case of guilt: I should be practicing my art, too. But I had nothing to say; like the world in the poem, I was dumb. The poem had to speak up for itself. It appropriated, along with the musician, my heart arrhythmia, which felt like an irate troll kicking me in the chest. Alarming but (I was told) harmless. The hospital monitor's transcription of the work of the heart fit with the theme of language, for our bodies speak to us constantly. Body language is everywhere: the planet uses it too.

"It's important to talk, especially when you have nothing to say, a friend newly in therapy told me. 'Semiotics' agrees wholeheartedly."

A. R. AMMONS was born on a farm outside Whiteville, North Carolina, in 1926. He started writing poetry aboard a U.S. Navy destroyer escort in the South Pacific. He worked briefly as the principal of an elementary school in Cape Hatteras and later managed a biological glass factory in southern New Jersey. Beginning in 1964 he taught at Cornell University, becoming the Goldwin Smith Professor of Poetry. He recently retired. He was awarded a MacArthur Fellowship in 1981, the year the "genius awards" were introduced. He has also received the Bollingen Prize (for *Sphere,* in 1975), the National Book Critics Circle Award (for *A Coast of Trees,* in 1981), and the National Book Award, twice—for *Collected Poems: 1951–1971* in 1973 and for the book-length poem *Garbage* in 1993. All these titles were published by Norton. Ammons's other books include *Ommateum* (1955), *Tape for the Turn of the Year* (1965), *The Snow Poems* (1977), *Worldly Hopes* (1982), *The Really Short Poems of A. R. Ammons* (1990), and *Glare* (1997). He was the guest editor of *The Best American Poetry 1994.* He and his wife live in Ithaca, New York.

Ammons notes: "The woman in 'Shot Glass' was a made-up person. Most of my poems are made-up. Some sound as if they're taken from reality, but I really just make them up. What's the use of being responsible for telling the truth all the time? The truth isn't always what's said but the way it's said. The title of this poem was meant to evoke the atmosphere of a bar scene and the effect on the speaker of a glass of whiskey."

JULIANNA BAGGOTT was born in Wilmington, Delaware, in 1969. She received her MFA in fiction from the University of North Carolina at Greensboro. Her first novel, *Girl Talk,* is to be published by Simon and Schuster's Pocket Books in January 2001, as well as by a number of overseas publishers. She started writing poetry a little over two years ago when her second child was six months old. Her poems have since been published in literary magazines such as *The Southern Review* and *Poetry.* Her collection of poems, *This Country of Mothers,* will be published by Southern Illinois University Press in April 2001. She lives in Newark, Delaware, with her husband, the poet David G. W. Scott, and their young children.

Of "Mary Todd on Her Deathbed," Baggott writes: "I'd heard, mistakenly, that Mary Todd Lincoln burned to death in an insane asylum where she was a patient. Fascinated, I began to research her life. At first glance, she is not a likable figure, and history hasn't been kind to her. But as I read, especially her insanity file now open to the public, I found a tragic life that ended in a darkened bedroom in her sister's house. In my poem, I've imagined her haunted by memories of being institutionalized, of her giant husband, her dead sons. Although I admit that I was initially drawn to her story because I was taken with the idea of writing her wild, fiery death, I found the way that she passed, slowly, nearly blind, her joints stiffening, to be achingly poetic."

ERIN BELIEU was born in 1966 and raised in Nebraska. She has writing degrees from Boston University and Ohio State University. Her first poetry collection, *Infanta* (Copper Canyon, 1995), was a selection of the National Poetry Series. Her second collection, *One Above & One Below* (Copper Canyon, 2000), was published last April. She has received a Rona Jaffe Foundation grant, an Ohio Arts Council award, and a St. Botolph Club Writers Award. She is currently at work coediting (with Susan Aizenberg) *The Extraordinary Tide: New Poetry by American Women* for Columbia University Press.

Belieu writes: "The impetus for 'Choose Your Garden' came from a visit I made to the botanical gardens in St. Louis. The visit occurred during a difficult time in my life—the specters of divorce, illness, and job insecurity were ganging up on me all at once—and it hit me as wonderfully absurd that I could come to such a place and be asked, quite literally, to choose my garden.

"Of course, as most grown-ups discover, choices are rarely what they seem to be on the surface, almost always disrupting one's tidy expectations. And, often, what appears to many to be the wrong choice for a person turns out to be the best thing that could have possibly happened. While these can be disconcerting notions to ponder, I also think recognizing one's absolute powerlessness to predict the 'right thing' can come as cosmic relief. I've decided the only thing to do is put on your best outfit, spin the wheel, and bet big. The sagest advice I ever received came from a friend's mother, a very wise woman from the Missouri Ozarks, who said, 'It's a good life if you don't give in. . . .' When I consider the alternative at which we all eventually arrive, I think she makes an excellent point."

RICHARD BLANCO was *made* in Cuba, *assembled* in Spain, and *imported* to the United States—meaning his mother, seven months pregnant, and the entire family arrived as exiles′ from Cienfuegos, Cuba, to Madrid where he was born. Only forty-five days later, the family immigrated once more and settled in Manhattan, then in Miami where Blanco was raised and educated. His résumé and interests are as diverse and read as colorfully as his background: professional engineer, translator, furniture designer, and YMCA volunteer. His first book of poetry, *City of a Hundred Fires,* won the Agnes Lynch Starrett Poetry Prize from the University of Pittsburgh. He describes himself as a builder of bridges and poems. He received both a B.S. degree in civil engineering (1991) and a M.F.A. in creative writing (1997) from Florida International University. He currently lives in Miami and in Connecticut, where he teaches creative writing and Latino/a Literature at Central Connecticut State University.

Of "Mango, Number 61," Blanco writes: "*La charada* is a sort of numerology by which objects and happenings are assigned numbers. For example, if on any given day my *abuela* would see a coconut fall, or a dead dog on the road, she'd yell out the corresponding number for *coco* or *perro muerto* and perhaps play the number in the lotto. As a child, I remember grown-ups randomly calling out numbers and sometimes arguing as to which number corresponded to which object. It was all very bizarre, since no one had ever bothered to explain *la charada*. As far as I could conceive, everything in the universe had a number, numbers

I did not know. The reason for 'Mango, Number 61' stems from these curious memories, and the significance I found later as an adult exploring my cultural circumstance and yearnings—the mix of myth and reason typical of my Hispanic heritage."

JANET BOWDAN was born in Chicopee, Massachusetts, in 1963. Her poems have appeared in *American Poetry Review, Colorado Review, Crazyhorse, Denver Quarterly, Hawai'i Review, Pavement Saw, Tinfish,* and *Verse.* She teaches at Western New England College in Springfield, Massachusetts.

Bowdan writes: "Two comments, really. The first is that I wrote 'The Year' after moving back to Massachusetts following a long time away, in Maryland and Colorado and England and, most recently, four years in central Louisiana. It was very odd to find myself meeting friends I hadn't seen for ages, completely by accident. I was thinking about this and about telling stories, wondering whether a happy ending was just a matter of where you chose to begin and end, so that you could create one if you tried.

"And the second is that the passion is in the shoes."

GRACE BUTCHER was born in Rochester, New York, in 1934. She moved to Ohio in 1941. A professor of English (emeritus) at Kent State University regional campuses, she has lived part-time in Chardon, Ohio, and part-time in Saskatoon, Saskatchewan, since 1993. Her books in print include *Child, House, World* (Hiram Poetry Review, 1991), *Before I Go Out on the Road* (Cleveland State University poetry series, 1979), *Rumors of Ecstasy . . . Rumors of Death* (Ashland University Press, 1971, rpt. Barnwood Press, 1981). Poetry and sports have been her lifelong focus: she has published in little magazines since the mid-sixties and has competed for fifty years at the national level in track, becoming U.S. champion and/or record holder in the 880/800 (1958–1961). She was a member of the AAU All-American, U.S. team that competed with the Soviets in 1959. She has held many titles and records in Masters (age group) track since 1977, including the world indoor record in the mile for women 60–65 in 1996. She founded and coached the running program at KSU Geauga Campus for twelve years and also founded the poetry workshop there. She raced motorcross and road-raced from 1974 to 1977, and wrote a column and feature stories on motorcycling for *Rider* magazine from 1979 to 1985. Her articles on track and motorcycling have appeared in *Runner's World* and *Sports Illustrated.*

Butcher writes: "'Crow Is Walking' is one of my own favorite poems. I've lived in the country most of my life and have always been intimately involved with the landscape around me. In recent years I learned that my grandmother's grandmother was Cree, and I seem to have been blessed with her Native American sense of how alive and how significant everything is in the natural world. One day while driving near home, I saw Crow (whom I've always thought of with a capital letter) walking down a dirt road as if he had somewhere to get to, and since it was such a nice day, he'd decided to walk. Where was he going? What was he thinking about? Since this poem, he's become a fairly major figure in other poems as well, often as a sort of philosopher with some insight to offer if I can be still, both physically and mentally, long enough to let myself learn what it is. In this poem he is trying several new things and will surely become a better Crow for the attempt."

LUCILLE CLIFTON was born in Depew, New York, in 1936. She served as poet laureate of the state of Maryland from 1975 to 1985. In 1999 she received a Lila Wallace–Reader's Digest Writers' Award. She has also received the Shelley Memorial Prize, an Emmy Award from the American Academy of Television Arts and Sciences, and a Lannan Achievement Award in poetry. She is currently Distinguished Professor of Humanities at St. Mary's College of Maryland. She has published ten collections of her poetry, one autobiographical prose work, and nineteen children's books, with more on the way. Her most recent publication, *The Terrible Stories,* was a finalist for the National Book Award, the Lenore Marshall Prize, and the *Los Angeles Times* Book Award. In May 1998, Slow Dancer Press published *The Terrible Stories* in England. She serves on the board of chancellors of the Academy of American Poets and was recently elected as a fellow of the American Academy of Arts and Sciences. Her next book, *Blessing the Boats: New and Selected Poems,* is due out from BOA Editions in April.

Of "Signs," Clifton writes: "This poem is composed of unusual things that I have seen . . . and that made me wonder, what do they mean? Often, when things are not acting according to what we think of as their nature, we not only wonder why, we also ask, 'Is this a sign? What does it mean?' I try to explore that a little in this poem."

BILLY COLLINS was born in New York City in 1941. His recent books include *Picnic, Lightning* (University of Pittsburgh Press, 1998), *The Art of Drowning* (University of Pittsburgh Press, 1995)—a finalist for the

Lenore Marshall Prize—and *Questions About Angels* (William Morrow, 1991), which was selected by Edward Hirsch for the National Poetry series and reprinted by the University of Pittsburgh Press in 1999. He has won the Bess Hokin Prize, the Levinson Prize, the Frederick Bock Prize, the Oscar Blumenthal Prize, and the Wood Prize—all awarded by *Poetry* magazine. A recipient of a Guggenheim fellowship and a grant from the National Endowment for the Arts, he is a professor of English at Lehman College (City University of New York) and a visiting writer at Sarah Lawrence College. He lives in northern Westchester County. His poems have appeared in the 1992 and 1993 editions of *The Best American Poetry* and in each of the last three books in the series.

Of "Man Listening to Disc," Collins writes: "I am usually not one of those people who walks around town with earphones on his head. I prefer to listen to the unpredictable noises of the city—people talking to themselves, a metal grate being thrown open, the sound of a messenger-bike with no brakes bearing down on me. But this day, I was wired to a metallic-blue Discman I had tucked in my coat pocket. The music ('Thelonious Monk/Sonny Rollins,' Prestige 7075) sounded so intimate and immediate as I walked up one street and down another, I could not help feeling that I was in the physical company of the musicians. And being wrapped in your own envelope of music *does* make you feel exceedingly egotistical. It is not hard to imagine that you are the star of your own private movie and that what you are listening to must be its sound track, the theme that always announces your momentous arrival on the scene.

"The poem came out easily enough, one musician at a time being acknowledged in an order determined by the size and weight of his instrument. Really, the hardest part of writing this one was making sure *Thelonious* was spelled correctly."

JIM DANIELS was born on June 6, 1956, in Detroit, Michigan. He is a professor of English at Carnegie Mellon University and lives with his wife, the writer Kristin Kovacic, and their two children, Ramsey and Rosalie, in Pittsburgh. He is the author of five books of poetry: *Blue Jesus* (Carnegie Mellon University Press, 2000), *Blessing the House* (University of Pittsburgh Press, 1997), *M-80* (University of Pittsburgh Press, 1993), *Punching Out* (Wayne State University Press, 1990), and *Places/Everyone* (University of Wisconsin Press; winner of the 1985 Brittingham Prize). In addition, he is the author of a collection of short stories, *No Pets* (Bottom Dog Press, 1999), and has edited or coedited the following anthologies: *American Poetry: The Next Generation* (Carnegie Mellon University Press, 2000), *Letters to America: Contemporary American Poetry on Race* (Wayne State University Press, 1995), and *The Carnegie Mellon Anthology of Poetry* (Carnegie Mellon University Press, 1993). (The first and third of these titles were edited in collaboration with Gerald Costanzo.) Daniels wrote the screenplay for "No Pets," a 1994 independent feature film directed by Tony Buba, and the one-act play, "Heart of Hearts," which was produced off-off Broadway in 1998. He has received a National Endowment for the Arts fellowship and two fellowships from the Pennsylvania Council for the Arts.

Of "Between Periods," Daniels writes: "As the father of two young children (ages three and two at the time of this poem), I was feeling invincible, full of their young lives, looking forward with exuberance and optimism. I remember Donald Hall's poem, 'My Son, My Executioner,' but I wasn't feeling that sense of mortality at the time—perhaps I was too busy changing diapers—but then I got one of those phone calls, and it happened to be on my birthday, so my own mortality whupped me upside the head. I had spent a year as a visiting professor at Florida International University while my wife worked at the Miami Book Fair. Debra was one of her coworkers there, and we'd become good friends during our year in Miami. We were living back in Pittsburgh when she called, so my wife and I felt even more helpless because of the physical distance between us and Debra.

"In my children's world, you can collect sunshine in baskets and wash your hands with air—the constant forward pull of life yanks us along even while we try to reach back and grieve for the losses. In the poem, I was trying to create that tension between moving forward and stopping by enjambing the stanzas, jumping around in time, and bringing in the world's interruptions. While any sports metaphor has become a cliché that prompts groans in our English department meetings, the idea of being 'between periods' seemed to work on a lot of levels for me here, and I couldn't not use it. This poem is in memory of Deborah Yagerman."

LINH DINH was born in Vietnam in 1963 and came to the United States in 1975. He now divides his time between the two countries. He is the author of a chapbook of poems, *Drunkard Boxing* (Singing Horse Press, 1998), and a collection of short stories, *Fake House* (Seven Stories Press, 2000). He is the editor of the anthology *Night, Again: Contemporary Fiction from Vietnam* (Seven Stories Press, 1996).

Dinh writes: "After reading 'The Most Beautiful Word,' a friend asked me if it had anything to do with my growing up in Vietnam during the war. I thought for a moment and said, 'What war?' The only casualties I saw growing up, aside from the black-and-white trophies laid out daily in the newspapers, were bodies lying prone after traffic accidents. (And the traffic situation in Saigon is still awful, let me tell you: folks don't stop at red lights and, just the other day, I saw a drunk fall off the backseat of a motorcycle. He bounced his face on the pavement then nearly choked on his own vomit, à la Jimi Hendrix.) The true genesis of this poem was a manual for field medics I bought at the U.S. government bookstore in Philly. (It's odd but each time I was in that fine bookstore, where you could buy anything from the CIA report on Botswana to the latest on Bull Run, I was the only customer.) The book cost me forty-five bucks and I hesitated before buying it because I wasn't sure I wanted to pay that much for a poem."

GREGORY DJANIKIAN was born in Alexandria, Egypt, in 1949, and came to the United States when he was eight years old. He is the author of four poetry collections: *The Man in the Middle* (1984), *Falling Deeply into America* (1989), *About Distance* (1995), and *Years Later* (2000), all published by Carnegie Mellon University Press. He teaches at the University of Pennsylvania and directs its undergraduate creative writing program.

Of "Immigrant Picnic," Djanikian writes: "Having spent the first half of their lives in Alexandria, Egypt, where many nationalities and languages flourished, my parents have often had trouble with American expressions. Our maternal language is Armenian, though my mother grew up speaking four others, and my father seven others, and sometimes, during conversations, two or three of them can make their way into the same sentence. It's a wonderful entertainment for the ear, and for the tongue as well if you're able to speak with their ease, though at times, because there are so many words to keep in mind, an expression such as 'he's a tall drink of water' may find itself altered to 'he's a thin drinking glass,' something a little odder though perhaps no less descriptive.

"This difficulty with idioms is mine as well, and I have to be especially careful of them out West where my wife was born and still has family and where Americanisms are as abundant as buffalo were once. It's a difficulty I try to overcome even though I have often mismanaged my own words until they've ridden off like wild horses, untethered and forever themselves. Which is to say that, for my family, a simple 'hello' from one to another may sometimes lead to syntactical surprises that, much to the horror of the parents, the dutiful son documents."

DENISE DUHAMEL was born in Providence, Rhode Island, in 1961, and grew up in Woonsocket, Rhode Island. She is the author of eleven books and chapbooks, the most recent of which are *The Star-Spangled Banner* (Southern Illinois University Press, 1999) and *Kinky* (Orchises Press, 1997). She has also collaborated extensively with the poet Maureen Seaton—in *Oyl* (Pearl Editions, 2000) and *Exquisite Politics* (Tia Chucha, 1997). Duhamel is married to the poet Nick Carbó and teaches in the MFA program at Florida International University in Miami.

Of "Incest Taboo," Duhamel writes: "I first heard a double sestina when Star Black read hers at the KGB Bar in New York City a few years ago. My poet friend Tom Fink had supplied me with the rules of the form a while earlier, and I would occasionally take sidelong glances at them, mostly in terror. I couldn't imagine sustaining such a long poem until I heard Star read hers. She gave me courage to try one myself. I took the double sestina rules with me to Villa Montalvo, an artists' colony I visited in May and June of 1998. After more than several false starts, I finished my first—'Incest Taboo.' Writing this poem, I felt as though I were doing a strenuous combination of math, crossword puzzles, and particle physics. Since then I've written several other double sestinas—'Hello Kitty,' 'The Brady Bunch,' and 'The Drag Queens Inside Me.' My head hasn't exploded yet."

CHRISTOPHER EDGAR was born in Pasadena, California, in 1961. He is publications director of Teachers & Writers Collaborative, a nonprofit arts organization in New York City. His poems have appeared in *Transfer, The Germ,* and *Shiny,* and he is an editor of *The Hat.* He translated *Tolstoy as Teacher: Leo Tolstoy's Writings on Education* (Teachers & Writers Collaborative, 2000) and has coedited a number of books on teaching writing, including *Classics in the Classroom: Using Great Literature to Teach Writing* (T&W, 1999). He lives in New York City.

Edgar writes: "'Birthday' began as a paean to my backyard as a kid, an expansive place of tree forts, manmade springs, and clubhouses full of jars marked 'XXX.' But the poem quickly got away from me. When I was ten or so, I spent a lot of time reading the encyclopedia (*S* was my favorite volume). I had a good memory for names, dates, and places, but I wasn't so good at context. (Around the time I wrote 'Birthday,' I was quite taken with an exhibition catalogue called *The Age of the Marvelous*, and I think I may have been imagining hazy parallels between my early book learning and the weird Renaissance collections of magical miscellany in the catalogue.) Anyhow, within a few lines the hodgepodge of information came swarming back, took the poem hostage, and carried it off, with this result."

KARL ELDER was born in Beloit, Wisconsin, in 1948. He is Lakeland College's Fessler Professor of creative writing. Four volumes of his poems have appeared from Prickly Pear Press, including *Phobophobia* (1987) and *A Man in Pieces* (1994). He has received the Lucien Stryk Award for poetry, grants from the Illinois Arts Council, and Lakeland's Outstanding Teacher Award. For several years he has edited the literary magazine *Seems*.

Elder writes: "I think of 'Alpha Images' as two-dimensional sculpture. Truthfully, I can't remember a lot about the composition of the sequence, probably because it's part of a much larger cycle of poems called *Locutions*. As I mentally walk through this room of the gallery, I'm reminded of the exquisite sense of excitement I had each time I cracked one of the visual codes. I believe I worked alphabetically, nearly a letter per day. 'A' was tough. I fought through countless drafts. But when I finished 'B,' I recognized *it* as the big battle won, the impetus to continue, although 'Z' resisted its seventeen syllables so severely that it became—naturally, I suppose—the poem's apocalypse."

LYNN EMANUEL was born in New York in 1949 and has lived, worked, and traveled in North Africa, Europe, and the Near East. She has degrees from Bennington College, the City College of New York, where she studied with Adrienne Rich, and the University of Iowa. She is the author of three books of poetry: *Hotel Fiesta, The Dig*, and *Then, Suddenly*—, all from the University of Pittsburgh Press. Her work was selected for *The Best American Poetry* in 1995 and 1998. She has been a poetry editor for the Pushcart Prize anthology, a member of the Literature Panel for the National Endowment for the Arts, and a judge for the James Laughlin Award from the Academy of American Poets. She has taught at the Bread Loaf Writers' Conference, the Bennington Writers' Workshops, and is currently a professor of English at the University of Pittsburgh, where she directs the writing program. She is married to the paleontologist Jeffrey Schwartz.

Lynn Emanuel writes: "As much as, or perhaps more than, a tribute to Whitman, 'Walt, I Salute You' is a tribute to the modernist Portuguese poet Fernando Pessoa and to his poem, 'Salutation to Walt Whitman.' Indeed, much of the over-the-top assonance and alliteration in my poem I've co-opted from Pessoa's 'Salutation.'

"Pessoa wrote under his own name in addition to using four 'heteronyms,' one of which was Alvaro de Campos, who is described by Pessoa as 'a naval engineer . . . 1.75 meters tall, two centimeters more than I, thin, with a tendency to a slight stoop . . . a vaguely Jewish, Portuguese type, hair therefore smooth and normally parted on the side, monocled.' Through the device of de Campos, Pessoa's 'Salutation' is hilariously funny, biting, and outrageous. It is not only an homage to and a critique of Whitman, but it is also a slyly brilliant political poem. Alvaro de Campos dissects Whitman in a startlingly contemporary way. He deconstructs Whitman's democratic spirit to reveal what he calls 'stampeding inspiration.' His Whitman is the devourer and exploiter of all that is not Whitman: 'The spirit giving life at this moment is ME! / Let no son of a bitch get in my way . . . / I feel the spurs, I am the horse I mount . . . / I can be everything . . . / Be the bitch to all dogs . . . / Be the steering wheel of all machines . . . / Be the one who's crushed, abandoned, pulled apart . . .'"

Editor's note: The inclusion of Emanuel's "Walt, I Salute You" marks the second time a poem inspired by Pessoa's "Salutation to Walt Whitman" has been chosen for *The Best American Poetry*. Allen Ginsberg's "Salutations to Fernando Pessoa" appeared in both the 1995 volume (edited by Richard Howard) and in Harold Bloom's selection of *The Best of the Best American Poetry 1988–1997*. A note in those volumes explains that a heteronym is not simply a pen name but a distinctive personality with a full life history.

B. H. FAIRCHILD was born in Houston, Texas, in 1942. He grew up in or around oil fields in west Texas, Oklahoma, and southwestern Kansas and has worked as a movie usher, machinist's helper, musician, and technical writer. He attended the University of Tulsa and University of Kansas. His books include *The Arrival of the Future* (Swallow's Tale Press, 1985), *The System of Which the Body Is One Part* (State Street Press, 1988), *Local Knowledge* (Quarterly Review of Literature, 1991), and *Such Holy Song* (Kent State University, 1980), a study of William Blake. His most recent book, *The Art of the Lathe* (Alice James Press, 1998), was a finalist for the National Book Award and received the William Carlos Williams

Award, the Kingsley Tufts Award, the PEN West Award, the California Book Award, and the Natalie Ornish Award from the Texas Institute of Letters. He has also received fellowships or grants from the Guggenheim Foundation, Rockefeller Foundation, and National Endowment for the Arts. He is currently professor of English at California State University–San Bernardino.

Fairchild writes: "'Mrs. Hill' began as a poem about Battle Creek, Michigan, from which my generation spent half its childhood waiting for packages to arrive, and drifted off into a memory of an actual incident that absolutely bewildered me as a child. That's what the poem is about, inasmuch as poems are about anything: a child's sense of bewilderment, chaos, meaninglessness in a world that promises meaning but never quite delivers."

CHARLES FORT was born in New Britain, Connecticut, in 1951. He holds the Reynolds chair in poetry and is professor of English at the University of Nebraska at Kearney. He has published poems in seventeen anthologies, including *The Best of Prose Poem International*. His books include *The Town Clock Burning* (St. Andrews Press, 1985, rpt. Carnegie Mellon University Press, 1991); *Darvil*, a prose poem sequence (St. Andrews Press, 1993); and *Brown Like a Father Close to Death* (1999) and *As the Lilac Burned the Laurel Grew* (1999), both from Reynolds Chair Books. He has received grants to complete a documentary on the lost factory tombs and brown fields of his hometown.

Fort writes: "'We Did Not Fear the Father' was completed in three years. The first year of drafts took the shape of a prose poem. The second year examined the form. There were shorter lines and stanzas in quatrains. I attempted to use the line *We did not fear the father* as the approximate line length of the entire work. The third year refined its metaphor, rhythm, and meter. I also used a longer line length: *We did not fear the father as the barber who stood,* and I found the emphasis I had originally sought in the shorter form remained. I also sustained the poem's unity and its narrative elements by using the phrase as a refrain.

There are two key transitions in the poem. (We did not fear the father *until he entered* the tomb of noise.) The ashes in the poem are lifted by love and fear. The son fears his father's weariness (We did not fear the father *until he stooped* in the dark) and mortality even as his father lifts his sons and daughters like birds into the top bunk beds. The time clock was a pendulum inside his father's heart that kept him alive. The father had a wife, seven children, a small black dog, grapevines, and a summer garden. The father was a workingman who toiled on the night shift grinding ball bearings in New Britain, Connecticut (once called the *Hardware City of the World*) from 11:00 A.M. to 7:00 A.M. for forty years. The father was a barber from 10:00 A.M. to 6:00 or 7:00 P.M., depending on the head count, for forty years. The father was a landlord in his three-story tenement house with attic apartments and on call twenty-four hours a day. I wanted to capture the three jobs he had as well as his forth and fifth: he was our father and the scare-monger."

FRANK X. GASPAR was born in Provincetown, Massachusetts, in 1946. His first collection of poems, *The Holyoke* (Northeastern University Press), won the 1988 Morse Prize for poetry. *Mass for the Grace of a Happy Death* (Anhinga Press) won the 1994 Anhinga Poetry Prize, and his third book, *A Field Guide to the Heavens* (University of Wisconsin Press) won the 1999 Brittingham Prize. A novel, *Leaving Pico,* was published in 1999 (Hardscrabble Books, University Press of New England) and received a Barnes & Noble Discover Award. His work has appeared in *The Best American Poetry 1996* as well as in *The Kenyon Review, The Georgia Review, The Harvard Review, The Gettysburg Review, Quarterly West,* and *The Bellingham Review.*

Gaspar writes: "'Seven Roses' is a meditation that begins with the experience of taking some breakfast after a long happy night of reading and writing. I don't remember the circumstances exactly, but I'm sure I began the poem right there at the table, over coffee, writing in one of my battered and often illegible notebooks. The piece pointedly avoids the conventions of the genteel gardening poem, but my expressed ambivalence toward yard work is genuine."

ELTON GLASER was born in New Orleans in 1945. He is Distinguished Professor Emeritus of English and former director of the University of Akron Press, where he still edits the Akron Series in Poetry. He has published four full-length collections of poems: *Relics* (Wesleyan University Press, 1984), *Tropical Depressions* (University of Iowa Press, 1988), *Color Photographs of the Ruins* (University of Pittsburgh Press, 1992), and *Winter Amnesties* (Southern Illinois University Press, 2000). He has won fellowships from the National Endowment for the Arts and the Ohio Arts Council. His poems have appeared in the 1995 and 1997 editions of *The Best American Poetry.*

Glaser writes: "'And in the Afternoons I Botanized' is a meditation in the form of a dialogue. The scene: a garden terrace in mid-October in the Midwest, late afternoon drifting into evening. The speakers: a middle-aged couple, cultured and self-aware, talking about the necessary extinction of the season and themselves. Their highly stylized conversation becomes a kind of elegy for the living, as they consider 'every hedge against death.' They imagine themselves as characters in various literary works, from Greek tragedies to the parlor verse of 'some teapot dame,' eventually realizing that no immortality can be found there, as even the most powerful language must finally fail: 'no words slow down the dirt.' Other possible solutions, religious and secular, are also rejected. Even love cannot save them. Confronted with the 'helpless evidence' of a waning world, they talk themselves into a corner from which there is no escape, where they have nothing left but each other and the inconsolable knowledge of their own end.

"And yet the poem itself almost belies these gloomy conclusions. Its lines are lively about death, buoyant on the undertow. Armed with jokes and puns and parodies, the poem behaves as if wit alone, with a rapier's edge and point, might be sharp enough to keep the Grim Reaper and his scythe at some defensible distance. And so it is. But not forever, not for long."

RAY GONZALEZ was born in El Paso, Texas, in 1952, and received an M.F.A. in creative writing from Southwest Texas State University in San Marcos, Texas. He is associate professor of English at the University of Minnesota, where he holds an endowed chair, The McKnight Land Grant Professorship. His poetry appeared in *The Best American Poetry 1999*, edited by Robert Bly, and in *The Pushcart Prize: Best of the Small Presses 2000* (Pushcart Press, 1999). He has written a memoir, *Memory Fever* (University of Arizona Press, 1999). His six books of poetry include *Cabato Sentora* (BOA Editions, 1999) and a prose poem memoir, *Turtle Pictures* (University of Arizona Press, 2000). Arizona will publish his first collection of fiction, *The Ghost of John Wayne and Other Stories,* in 2001, and his second book of essays, *The Underground Heart: Essays from Hidden Landscapes,* in 2002. He has served as poetry editor of *The Bloomsbury Review* for twenty years and is the editor and publisher of *LUNA: A New Journal of Poetry and Translations.*

Gonzalez writes: "'For the Other World' is a poem about cultural and family secrets—those hidden worlds where individuals swallow the past without thinking it will come back to haunt them. To write the poem is to say there is the voice of the poet writing from far away, a vision he had as a child, making him put it all down. It is also a poem about labor—the dark habits of husbands and wives who come home late from work without having much to say to each other—the young boy the real witness to their silence. The final image of sweat is the common sign of reaffirmation after this entire history has been acknowledged, re-created, and left on the page for those willing to nod their heads in their own silence."

JENNIFER GROTZ was born in Canyon, Texas, in 1971, and attended the same high school as Buddy Holly in Lubbock. She studied French, English, and art history at Tulane University and at the Université de Paris. In 1996 she received her MFA in poetry and MA in English from Indiana University in Bloomington. She has received scholarships and awards from Oregon Literary Arts, Bread Loaf Writers' Conference, and the National Society of Arts and Letters. Her poems have appeared in *TriQuarterly, Ploughshares, Black Warrior Review,* and *New England Review.* She works as the office manager at Mountain Writers Series and serves as an adjunct faculty member of Mt. Hood Community College in Portland, Oregon. She has completed a manuscript of poems, *Cusp.*

Grotz writes: "'The Last Living Castrato' came from learning two interesting pieces of history on the same day. One was that when Thomas Edison first learned how to record sound on wax cylinders, he traveled around and captured important voices of his time. Wax cylinders still remain that capture Walt Whitman reading and the last living castrato singing, among other voices. The second fact I learned was that because castrati were common in opera history, many roles were written for voices capable of spanning up to eight octaves. 'The Last Living Castrato' is a poetic meditation on those facts. It is also my homage to the voice. I am fascinated by past (clearly abhorrent) sacrifices made in European musical history to achieve this extraordinary voice. It seems to me that these castrati were poets of a sort, über-voice speaking beyond gender to a kind of soul. Even Edison's wax cylinders seem voicelike in their malleability. To play them is also to damage them, and the voice of the castrato has some similar dynamic, that its beauty is also a marker of cruelty or damage.

"Shortly after writing this poem, I had the pleasure of seeing an opera composed for castrati, Handel's *Agrippina,* performed at Indiana University. As the conventionally male roles were required to sing in a high register and some of the female voices were required to sing low, the casting was wonderfully gender-crossed, replete with men singing in dresses and women singing as male characters. Half the pleasure of the opera, which is actually pretty long and tedious, was witnessing how the directors overcame the original intentions of the work."

THOM GUNN was born in England in 1929. He came to California in 1954 and has lived in San Francisco for many years. His first book was published in 1954. His recent books of poetry include *The Man with Night Sweats* (1992), *Collected Poems* (1994), and the forthcoming *Boss Cupid,* all from Farrar, Straus and Giroux. *The Occasions of Poetry,* comprising essays in criticism and autobiography, is back in print from the University of Michigan Press. In 1993 he was named a MacArthur Fellow. He has retired after teaching for many years at Berkeley.

Of "The Dump," Gunn writes: "The poet in question is a composite. When Allen Ginsberg's 'papers' were sold to Stanford University, I read that they included every pair of sneakers he had ever owned. Like a saint's relics. (What a hoarder he must have been!) Yet the poem is not about Ginsberg, it's about missing the point. My moral is crudely obvious."

MARK HALLIDAY was born in 1949 in Ann Arbor, Michigan. He directs the creative writing program at Ohio University. His books of poems are *Little Star* (William Morrow, 1987), *Tasker Street* (University of Massachusetts, 1992), and *Selfwolf* (University of Chicago, 1999). His critical study, *Stevens and the Interpersonal,* was published by Princeton in 1991. He resents the way things done in the late twentieth century will soon seem to be "back then."

Halliday writes: "'Before' tries to express the sense of how other people complicate oneself. Years pass, imposing layer upon layer of nuance in the way we respond to each new other. The kind of fatigue that results is indispensable and often sweet."

BARBARA HAMBY was born in New Orleans in 1952 and, because her father was in the air force, spent her childhood in many places, including France, Virginia, and Hawai'i. Her first book, *Delirium* (University of North Texas), won the 1994 Vassar Miller Prize, the 1996 Kate Tufts Discovery Award, and the Poetry Society of America's Norma Farber First Book Prize. In 1996 she received a National Endowment for the Arts Poetry Fellowship. Her second book, *The Alphabet of Desire,* appeared in 1999 from New York University Press. She lives in Tallahassee, Florida, with her husband, the poet David Kirby.

Of "Ode to the Lost Luggage Warehouse at the Rome Airport,"
Hamby writes: "In 1992, my husband and I lived for five months in Flo-
rence, Italy, a trip we had planned for some time and which I had fan-
tasized about even longer. Every fantasy starred me, of course, wearing
my most beautiful clothes and shoes, and looking more like Ava Gard-
ner in her twenties than me as a forty-year-old. As we age and the body
begins its ritual betrayal, looking marvelous becomes a dicier endeavor.
One of my pet obsessions is with my triceps (aka Ethel Mermans), since
I look exactly like my grandmother who died at ninety-three without
her mind and with Ethel Mermans the size of huge swinging Virginia
hams. I suppose I feel helpless in the face of dementia, but my arms—
maybe I can do something about them. For the trip I packed all my ball-
gowns and tiaras and also included two dumbbells so I could continue
my upper arm regime. Guess who was the real dumbbell here, because
the weights must have looked like bombs in the airport X ray, and my
bag never left the Miami terminal. Meanwhile our house sitter, instead
of forwarding our mail *via aerea,* sent it by the slow boat to save us
money, so I didn't receive the notice about my bag from Miami for three
months. For three months, then, I was occupied in a hideous roundelay
with Alitalia from which 'Ode to the Lost Luggage Warehouse at the
Rome Airport' was born. A couple of years later, I was in love with
Dante and wanted to write my very own poem in terza rima about a visit
to hell. The lost luggage warehouse at the Rome airport was pretty
hellish, so I had my subject, and the first version of the poem was in
terza rima. But it really didn't work, so I put the poem away, not know-
ing how to fix it or if I could. In the meantime I started working on a
series of odes, many of which were set in Italy to which we returned in
1994 and 1996. One day I remembered the Rome airport poem, pulled
it apart, and reconfigured it as an ode. I loved Paul Valéry's aphorism,
'God made the world from nothing, and sometimes the nothing shows
through.' Sometimes I think the terza rima shows through in this ode.
I don't know why that makes me happy, but it does."

FORREST HAMER was born in Goldsboro, North Carolina, in 1956, and
currently lives in Oakland, California, where he is a psychologist, a
candidate psychoanalyst and a lecturer at the University of California,
Berkeley. He was educated at Yale and Berkeley and is the author of
Call & Response (Alice James, 1995), winner of the Beatrice Hawley
Award, and *Middle Ear,* which is under editorial review. His work was
chosen for *The Best American Poetry 1994.*

Of "Goldsboro Narratives," Hamer writes: "These narratives come from a sequence of poems about the nature of psychic location—geographical place as psychological space, relations with others as these locate a self, that self as historical narrative. I'm particularly interested in the influence of childhood on feeling located and related. The Goldsboro narratives were inspired most by William Carlos Williams's *Paterson,* a collection I was introduced to as a college freshman a long way away from home."

BRENDA HILLMAN was born in Tucson, Arizona, in 1951. After receiving her BA at Pomona College, she traveled extensively and then attended the University of Iowa, where she received her MFA in 1976. She has worked at several jobs but mostly as a teacher; at present she is on the faculty of St. Mary's College in Moraga, California, where she teaches in the undergraduate and graduate programs, and serves on the permanent faculties of Squaw Valley Community of Writers and of Napa Valley Writers' Conference. Her five collections of poetry—*White Dress* (1985), *Fortress* (1989), *Death Tractates* (1992), *Bright Existence* (1993) and *Loose Sugar* (1997)—have been published by Wesleyan University Press; she has also written two chapbooks, *Coffee, 3 AM* (Penumbra Press, 1982) and *Autumn Sojourn* (Em Press, 1995). She has edited an edition of Emily Dickinson's poetry for Shambhala Publications, and, with Patricia Dienstfrey, has coedited *New Writings on Poetics and Motherhood.* She resides in the San Francisco Bay Area, is married, and has a daughter.

Of "Air for Mercury," Hillman writes: "Of course, what I intended is irrelevant. I had hoped to play with metaphors for the artist's relationship to a life of service in places of political or natural power. The couplet form seemed intimate. The title occurred when I misread a license plate while running. I had given myself an assignment to count numbers of words per lines, and to make rapid shifts in types of reality."

MARSHA JANSON was born in Attleboro, Massachusetts, in 1956. She holds a degree from Smith College and has studied theology at Harvard Divinity School. Her poems have been published in *Harvard Review, Prairie Schooner, Many Mountains Moving, Cream City Review, Salamander, The Worcester Review,* and *Peregrine.* She is a founder of the North Shore Workshop for Emerging Writers and is employed as a community health nurse in the field of mental health. She lives north of Boston with her husband and daughter.

Of "Considering the Demise of Everything," Janson writes: "There wasn't much in the way of intention in the writing of this poem. The process was kind of like falling backwards Alice-like down the rabbit hole. A friend used the trigger 'thank you' in a writing exercise and some unexpected things flew in. The last nine lines had their origin in time spent traveling in the Southwest; a stream-of-consciousness contemplation of the sometimes brief meetings with things and events that for no obvious reason leave an imprint. At work in the poem is the poet's encounter with herself and with the notion of impermanence. In an earlier version the canary was a hummingbird."

MARK JARMAN was born in Mount Sterling, Kentucky, in 1952. He is the author of seven books of poetry: *North Sea* (Cleveland State University Poetry Center, 1978), *The Rote Walker* (Carnegie Mellon University Press, 1981), *Far and Away* (Carnegie Mellon University Press, 1985), *The Black Riviera* (Wesleyan University Press, 1990), *Iris* (Story Line Press, 1992), *Questions for Ecclesiastes* (Story Line Press, 1997), and *Unholy Sonnets* (Story Line Press, 2000). *The Black Riviera* won the 1991 Poets' Prize. *Questions for Ecclesiastes* won the 1998 Lenore Marshall Poetry Prize from the Academy of American Poets and *The Nation* magazine. With Robert McDowell, he is the coauthor of *The Reaper Essays* (Story Line Press, 1996), and with David Mason, he has edited *Rebel Angels: 25 Poets of the New Formalism* (Story Line Press, 1996). His book of essays, *The Secret of Poetry,* is forthcoming. He is a professor of English at Vanderbilt University in Nashville, Tennessee.

Jarman writes: "'Epistle' is one of a series of prose poems I have been trying to write, based on the manner in which St. Paul speaks to the early Christians, providing them with ways to think about their faith. My hope in the series is to create metaphors for belief and faith that will be religious without being sectarian, heterodox rather than orthodox. St. Paul, a maker of vivid metaphors, writes in his Epistle to the Hebrews (4:12): 'For the word of God is quick, and powerful, and sharper than any two-edged sword, piercing even to the dividing asunder of soul and spirit, and of the joints and marrow, and is a discerner of the thoughts and intents of the heart.' My aim in 'Epistle' is to take St. Paul more literally, perhaps, than he intended."

PATRICIA SPEARS JONES was born in Forrest City, Arkansas, in 1951. She moved to New York City in 1974 and worked with a theater company (Mabou Mines), worked in day-care centers, then got a real job at Samuel French. She participated in Lewis Warsh's workshops at the St.

Mark's Poetry Project. She produced a mimeo magazine, *W. B.*, in 1975, and coedited *Ordinary Women*. She lives in Brooklyn, New York.

Of "Ghosts," Jones writes: "The poem is an appreciation of the legend of Albert Ayler, whose name was often attached to critical reviews of David Murray, a young tenor player who became a great friend of mine in the mid-seventies during the Loft Jazz era. I had a lover, who had been friends with both Charlie Parker and Ayler, and the poem quotes his memories. But mostly 'Ghosts' is about Second Avenue, a fabled street in New York Bohemia. I chose couplets to give the poem a formal feel and to slow the pace. I wanted to honor Ayler's music without trying to imitate his tone; I'd read too many bad Coltrane poems in which the poet desperately tries to match Trane's complexities and winds up with a simplistic love-peace-and-understanding tone. Finally, 'Ghosts' is a salutation to youthful desire and promise. Sometimes your dreams do come true and sometimes you drop dead in the water."

RODNEY JONES was born in Hartselle, Alabama, in 1950. He grew up on a farm near Falkville, Alabama, then studied at the University of Alabama and the University of North Carolina at Greensboro. He is the author of six books of poetry: *The Story They Told Us of Light* (University of Alabama Press, 1980); *The Unborn* (Atlantic Monthly Press, 1985); and *Transparent Gestures* (1989), *Apocalyptic Narrative* (1993), *Things that Happen Once* (1996), and *Elegy for the Southern Drawl* (1999), all from Houghton Mifflin. He has received a Guggenheim Fellowship, the Jean Stein Award from the American Academy of Arts and Letters, and the National Book Critics Circle Award. He teaches in the creative writing program at Southern Illinois University at Carbondale.

DONALD JUSTICE was born in Miami, Florida, in 1925, and currently resides in Iowa. For his poetry he has received the Pulitzer Prize, the Bollingen Prize, and, in 1996, the Lannan Literary Award. His recent books include *New and Selected Poems* (Knopf, 1995), *Orpheus Hesitated Beside the Black River* (Anvil Press [UK], 1998) and *Oblivion* (Story Line Press, 1998), a book of criticism. He also paints and composes music.

Of "Ralph: A Love Story," Justice writes: "The poem comes from an old family story, told rarely and, as I recall, in whispers. I may have got it wrong but there is no one else alive to improve on my version. Ralph himself, incidentally, stopped going to movies altogether about the time talkies were coming in."

OLENA KALYTIAK DAVIS, born in Detroit in 1963, is the author of *And Her Soul Out of Nothing* (Wisconsin, 1997). She is momentarily living in the Bay Area with her husband and newborn son, and not working on completing her second manuscript, *Shattered Sonnets Love Cards and Other Off and Back-handed Importunities.*

Kalytiak Davis writes: "'Six Apologies, Lord' wrote itself while I was working a relief shift at the Juneau Public Library circulation desk. Unfortunately, the texts it was stolen from were not the texts that circulated frequently. Though it's hard to tell out of context, 'Six Apologies' is one of a series, or should I say sequence, of 'Shattered Sonnets' that sort of simultaneously distort, discard, and highlight formal, thematic, and rhetorical sonnet conventions.

"Oh yeah, and I needed to say I was sorry."

DAVID KIRBY was born in Baton Rouge, Louisiana, in 1944. He is currently the W. Guy McKenzie Professor of English at Florida State University. His books of poetry include *Big-Leg Music, My Twentieth Century,* both from Orchises Press, and most recently *The House of Blue Light* (LSU Press, 2000). He is married to the poet Barbara Hamby and lives in Tallahassee, Florida.

Of "At the Grave of Harold Goldstein," Kirby writes: "A few years ago, I got tired of reading (and writing) the 2" x 4" I-looked-out-my-window-and-here's-what-I-saw poem and decided to let the poems be as long as they wanted to and say whatever they needed to say. I was influenced by the poet David Antin but also by monologist Spalding Gray and cartoonist Stan Mack, whose *Village Voice* cartoons about New York street life were always accompanied by the tag line, 'Guaranteed: All Dialogue Reported Verbatim.' Mainly, I was trying to do what Whitman does and offer a first-person speaker as a proxy for all humanity. I decided to counter the looseness of the poems' contents with a saw-toothed stanza I was pretty proud of until I opened the *Norton Anthology* one day to teach Marianne Moore to a roomful of sophomores and blushed when I realized she had beaten me to it. Ah, well, no new thing under the sun, as Ecclesiastes says.

"The first of my memory poems were chronological reports, but then the poems began to get almost Talmudic in character as I incorporated others' stories, snippets of things I'd read, commentary, commentary on commentary, and so on. Reviewing an anthology I was in, Judith Kitchen referred to 'David Kirby's hilarious roundabout forays into his own mind,' a humbling reminder that someone else can usually describe what you're doing better than you can. Let me close on an inspirational note: before 'At the Grave of Harold Goldstein' was accepted by *Parnassus,* it was turned down by seventeen magazines. So you poets, hang in there."

CAROLYN KIZER was born in Spokane in 1925 and was educated at Sarah Lawrence College and Columbia University. She spent a year in China, and twenty years later, a year in Pakistan. With Richard Hugo she founded the quarterly *Poetry Northwest,* which she edited until becoming the first Director of Literature for the National Endowment for the Arts, from 1965 until 1970. She resigned when the Chairman of the N.E.A., Roger Stevens, was fired by President Nixon. She then went to the University of North Carolina, where she reorganized the poetry program. She has taught at many universities, including Columbia, Princeton, and Stanford. Her book of poems, *YIN,* won the Pulitzer Prize in 1985. She was made a Chancellor of the Academy of American Poets in 1995 but resigned four years later because of the Chancellors' neglect of ethnic and geographic diversity—a situation since greatly improved. She has published seven books of poetry, two books of criticism and a book of translations. She has edited *The Essential John Clare* and *100 Great Poems by Women.* Her most recent book is *Harping On: Poems 1985–1995.* She and her husband live in Sonoma, California, and spend part of each year in Paris.

Of "The Oration," Kizer writes: "My cherished friend, Edmund ('Mike') Keeley, the renowned translator of modern Greek poetry, told me he was collecting poems by American poets who had been influenced by Constantine Cavafy. I had always cared deeply for Cavafy, but I had never modeled a poem on him. So now I did. My first effort was a close imitation, called 'Days of 1986' (a number of poets have used variants on this particular poem's title and content). But on thinking about it, I realized that one of his most characteristic innovations was to write about an important historical or mythical event or person from the standpoint of an insignificant person, a bystander, 'an attendant lord.' So that was the usage I adopted in writing 'The Oration.' When I wrote that the poem was 'after Cavafy' I was rather shocked when the editor of the *Threepenny Review,* who conditionally accepted the poem, inquired if 'after Cavafy' meant that it was a translation! I replied that 'after' meant 'in the style of.' I had thought that every literary person accepted that. Anyway, she printed it.

"Another remarkable thing about Cavafy's poems is the absence of specific metaphors. There is an overriding metaphor in most of the poems: the comparison of what *was* with what *is*. I've always been drenched in metaphor—although wary of the word 'like.' So now, having immersed myself in Cavafy yet again, I shall try to be stingy with metaphors. At any rate, my warm thanks to Mike Keeley for translating Cavafy in the first place and for stimulating me to write these poems."

LYNNE KNIGHT was born in Philadelphia, Pennsylvania, in 1943, and grew up in Cornwall-on-Hudson, New York. She graduated from the University of Michigan, where she won two Hopwood awards, and from Syracuse University, where she was a fellow in poetry. After living for several years in Canada, where her daughter was born, she moved to upstate New York and taught high school English for a number of years. In 1990 she moved to Berkeley, California. Her first collection, *Dissolving Borders,* won a Quarterly Review of Literature prize in 1996. She teaches writing at two Bay Area community colleges.

Of "The Muse of the Actual," Knight writes: "After a long period of not writing poems, I attended a National Endowment for the Humanities seminar on Joyce's *Ulysses* at Cornell during the summer of 1987. There I met the poet Nan Farady, who became a dear friend, and who encouraged me to start writing poems again. In the years after the seminar we would sometimes steal days from our teaching jobs and meet in Ithaca to talk about poems and men—about art and the actual. Nan would have laughed at the notion of a muse of the actual, as she would have laughed at the failed metamorphosis of the painted bull. She loved humor that turned on irony.

"When Nan died in 1996, a hard death that came far too soon, I found myself writing poem after poem in mourning. Slowly I worked my way back to poems like this one, less in elegy, more in celebration of her life and spirit. She had a wonderful capacity to see things as they actually are and yet to insist on a deeply romantic view of life. Both of these, I discovered in writing the poem, were aspects of her generosity. She knew very well which version would prevail, but she forgave the world (and her mother) as she forgave the painter. And right up to the end, she went on hoping."

YUSEF KOMUNYAKAA was born in Bogalusa, Louisiana, in 1947. His most recent books include *Talking Dirty to the Gods* (poems, Farrar, Straus and Giroux) and *Blue Notes: Essays, Interviews and Commentaries* (Poets on Poetry Series, University of Michigan Press), both in 2000.

Among his other titles are *Thieves of Paradise,* a finalist for the 1999 National Book Critics Circle Award, and *Neon Vernacular: New and Selected Poems 1977–1989,* winner of the 1994 Pulitzer Prize in poetry. Forthcoming is *Pleasure Dome: New and Collected Poems, 1975–1999* (Wesleyan, spring 2001). He wrote the lyrics for *Thirteen Kinds of Desire* (Cornucopia Productions, 2000), sung by jazz singer Pamela Knowles. Elected to the Board of Chancellors of the Academy of American Poets in 1999, he teaches at Princeton University.

Of "The Goddess of Quotas Laments," Komunyakaa writes: "A few years before George Wallace died, I found myself standing in the campus of the University of Alabama at Tuscaloosa, realizing the parallel etymology of Bogalusa, where I was born in Louisiana, and also keenly aware of that former governor and presidential candidate who received millions of votes across America. At least, for me, his presence was there that sunny day in 'Dixie' (wasn't this song written by a New Yorker?); and I wondered how some people in Alabama had risen with grace to forgive him. Wallace had positioned himself in the entranceway of the university, as if to say, 'Over my dead body.'

"Yet, today, ironically when I think about the Deep South, I find myself comparing Bull Connors with recent acts by officials in the northeast and the west. More progress between the races has been made in the south than elsewhere in this country (one has only to think of Bill Clinton). George Wallace found himself recanting his overt bigotry. But still his past actions had perversely helped to nourish a demented seed in the psyche. This goddess laments the counterinstinctive embedded so deeply that nature has been affected, almost as if a mental illness had been inherited and passed down. It is like some classical curse where the dead return repeatedly to haunt the living."

THOMAS LUX was born in Northampton, Massachusetts, in 1946. He was raised on a small family dairy farm. After attending Emerson College in Boston, he spent a year at the Iowa Writers' Workshop, then returned to Emerson to teach. He has taught at Sarah Lawrence College since 1975. He has received a Guggenheim Fellowship and has held National Endowment for the Arts fellowships three times. His most recent books are *Split Horizon* (Houghton Mifflin, 1994), *Selected Poems: 1975–1995* (Houghton Mifflin, 1997), and *The Blind Swimmer: Selected Early Poems, 1970–1975* (Adastra, 1996). He has stated his belief that people hunger for "what poetry, at its best, provides: something both complex and simple, something human and alive, something rarely overproduced but not lacking in its own kind of pyrotechnics. A lot of us feel overwhelmed in our lives by a popular culture dominated by technology, hugely overproduced movies and music. Poets have only one instrument. There are no backup singers for poets, no props, no synthesizers, no special effects. Just pure lucid words. Put in the proper order—which includes the order of their sounds—they can shake us to the bones." He was the guest editor of a recent (1999) issue of *Ploughshares,* in which the quoted sentences appear.

LYNNE MCMAHON was born in Marshalltown, Iowa, in 1951. Her new book of poems, *The House of Entertaining Science,* is available from David R. Godine. She is a professor at the University of Missouri, Columbia.

Of "We Take Our Children to Ireland," McMahon writes: "The poem is so narratively detailed it says everything right up front—no layers of ambiguity at all."

W. S. MERWIN was born in New York City in 1927, and grew up in Union City, New Jersey, and in Scranton, Pennsylvania. From 1949 to 1951 he worked as a tutor in France, Portugal, and Majorca, and later earned his living by translating from the French, Spanish, Latin, and Portuguese. He has also lived in England and in Mexico. *A Mask for Janus,* his first book of poems, was chosen by W. H. Auden as the 1952 volume in the Yale Series of Younger Poets. Subsequent volumes include *The Moving Target* (1963), *The Compass Flower* (1977), and *The Rain in the Trees* (Knopf, 1988). *The Carrier of Ladders* (1970) won the Pulitzer Prize. He has translated *The Poem of the Cid* and *The Song of Roland,* and his *Selected Translations 1948–1968* won the PEN Translation Prize for 1968. His recent books are *Travels* (1993), *The Vixen* (1996), *The Folding Cliffs* (1998), and *The River Sound* (1999), all from Knopf. *East Window,* comprising his translations of poems, appeared from Copper Canyon Press in 1998. He was the first recipient of the Dorothea Tanning Prize from the Academy of American Poets in 1994. Later that year he won a three-year writer's award from the Lila Wallace–Reader's Digest Fund. He lives in Hawaii—in a place called Haiku, on the island of Maui.

Merwin writes: "'The Hours of Darkness' is one of a number of recent poems directed toward the relation between light and darkness."

SUSAN MITCHELL grew up in New York City and was educated at Wellesley College. Her most recent book of poems is *Erotikon* (HarperCollins,

2000). Her previous book, *Rapture* (HarperCollins, 1992), was a National Book Award finalist and winner of the Kingsley Tufts Poetry Award. She has received fellowships from the Guggenheim Foundation, the Lannan Foundation, and the National Endowment for the Arts. She is a professor in the graduate creative writing program at Florida Atlantic University and divides her time between Boca Raton, Florida, and Washington, Connecticut.

Mitchell writes: "'Lost Parrot' came to me very fast, its rhymes and structure almost immediately what they are now. How does it happen that a poem grows and develops in the dark of the poet's mind? All I can say is it is one of the mysteries of poetry writing that gives me tremendous pleasure. In folktales, animal helpers perform feats impossible for the human hero or heroine. Those ants in the story of Amor and Psyche, for example, how quickly they sort the mountain of seeds and grains that had left Psyche dumbfounded and dismayed. I like to think of such animal helpers as metaphors for powers and forces within our own minds, energies able to perform complicated tasks with amazing speed."

JEAN NORDHAUS was born in Baltimore, Maryland, in 1939, studied philosophy at Barnard College and received her doctorate in modern German literature from Yale University. Her most recent books of poems are *My Life in Hiding,* which appeared in fall 1991 in the *Quarterly Review of Literature, Vol. XXX,* and *The Porcelain Apes of Moses Mendelssohn,* which appeared in Jerusalem in 1996 in a Hebrew translation by the Israeli poet Moshe Dor. A chapbook version of this manuscript, *A Purchase of Porcelain,* was published in 1998. She is also the author of two earlier volumes of poetry, *A Bracelet of Lies* (Washington Writers' Publishing House, 1987) and a chapbook, *A Language of Hands* (SCOP, 1982).

Of "Aunt Lily and Frederick the Great," Nordhaus writes; "I had been working for some months on a book-length series of poems about Moses Mendelssohn, the first Jew to publish a book in the German language and an important figure in both the German and Jewish Enlightenment. As a young man, Mendelssohn was part of a group promoting the literary use of German at a time when most educated Germans— including Frederick the Great—wrote in French. Mendelssohn published an unfavorable review of a book of Frederick's French poetry, and Frederick later retaliated by tabling Mendelssohn's nomination to the Royal Academy.

"I felt that I needed to include a poem about Frederick the Great in my series, but at the time, I knew very little about him, other than that he wrote music and poetry, founded the German Academy, had a palace called Sans Souci, and was a serious Francophile. It so happens that my Aunt Lily was also a francophile, and so the title, 'Aunt Lily and Frederick the Great' popped into my head.

"The poem turned out to be less about Frederick the Great than about Aunt Lily, and less about Lily herself than about the way history plays itself out not only through the actions and decisions of the 'great' (as we are so often taught) but also in the lives of ordinary people."

MARY OLIVER was born in Ohio in 1935. She currently holds the Catharine Osgood Foster Chair for Distinguished Teaching at Bennington College. She received the Pulitzer Prize for *American Primitive* (1984) and the National Book Award for her *New and Selected Poems* (1992). Her most recent book is *Winter Hours,* which includes essays, poems, and prose poems. "Work" is one of seven poems that will combine to form her next book, *The Leaf and the Cloud,* to be published by Da Capo Press in fall 2000. She lives in Provincetown, Massachusetts, and in Bennington, Vermont.

Of "Work," Oliver writes: "Most of the poems I read these days— and most of the poems I myself have written—seem to me to be beset by two elements: the wish to be a little 'snappy' in terms of language, and the wish to deal with certainties or what might be called 'answers' in opposition to 'questions.' Yet most of life (including the inner language life) is about questions, and is snappy only at the rare moment of sarcasm or wit. Mostly, we go on and on, an energy that does not ever take us home directly, but swirls and encircles and delays and prolongs us—through doubt, through passion, through examples of all kinds— to the end, at least for the moment, of *that* conversation. 'Work' is one such conversation. Of course I don't mean by what I have said that it wasn't *written,* and rewritten and rewritten many times. I mean only that I refused to let either a wish to be stylish in a succinct way or a desire to stop where one might lean against some small answer curtail the ongoing flow of the poem and (there are seven such poems) the book."

MICHAEL PALMER was born in New York City in 1943 and has lived in San Francisco since 1969. He has published nine collections of poetry. He has worked extensively with contemporary dance, in various modes of collaboration, for over twenty years, and has also collaborated with numerous visual artists and composers. His most recent collections are *At Passages* (New Directions, 1995) and *The Lion Bridge (Selected Poems 1972–1995)* (New Directions, 1998). With Régis Bonvicino and Nelson Ascher, he recently edited and helped to translate *Nothing the Sun Could Not Explain: 20 Contemporary Brazilian Poets* (Sun & Moon Press, 1997). A new collection of poetry, *The Promises of Glass,* will appear in spring 2000 from New Directions. In September 1999, a prose work, *The Danish Notebook,* was published by Avec Books.

Of "I Do Not," Palmer writes: "Some time ago, the French poet Emmanuel Hocquard sent me his reprint of Georges Hugnet's preface to Hugnet's 1922 translation of selected passages from Gertrude Stein's *The Making of Americans.* The preface begins with the following two sentences:

Je ne sais pas l'anglais.

Je ne sais pas l'anglais mais j'ai traduit lettre par lettre et virgule
      par virgule.

Immediately I felt that I was being given both the start of a poem (poem as natural home of Monsieur, or is it Madame, Paradoxe) and its essential prose-poetry cadence, one that would carry me through to the end, though I couldn't of course envision that end. The 'war' mentioned is our renewed bombing of Iraq, with the usual, tightly controlled images supplied to an ever-gullible &/or servile media. For the Antioch College 'protocol' (the 'Antioch Ruling') on sexual conduct, I am indebted to an anecdote in the novelist Siri Hustvedt's cogent and engaging essay 'The Tears of Eros,' from her collection *Yonder* (Henry Holt, 1998). And so the hall of mirrors constructs itself, fragment by fragment, necessity and chance doing their dance."

PAUL PERRY was born in Dublin, Ireland, in 1972. He was educated at Brown University and at Trinity College in Dublin and was a James Michener Fellow at the University of Miami, where he received his MFA in 1995. In 1998 he was awarded the Hennessy Prize for Irish Literature. His first book of poetry, *The Drowning of the Saints,* is forthcoming from Salmon Books. Currently, he is a C. Glenn Cambor Fellow at the University of Houston.

Perry writes: "'Paris' is an homage to Paul Celan, a poet whose work

I first encountered in the German school I attended in Dublin. Having made regular trips to Germany over the years and studied German literature and language, I found myself rewriting lines from Celan's poems, translating, mistranslating, 'imitating' in a Lowell-like way and deriving my own work from those mysterious poems in an effort I suppose to enter into some kind of understanding with the words of the poet. The result is a pantoum, a form I chose for the recurring lines, the haunting revisitations and revisions that I found my own process in understanding poems and making poems took."

CARL PHILLIPS, born in Washington in 1959, is the author of four books of poetry, including *Pastoral* (Graywolf Press, 2000). *Cortège* was a finalist for the 1995 National Book Critics Circle Award, and *From the Devotions,* a finalist for the 1998 National Book Award. The recipient of fellowships and awards from the Guggenheim Foundation, the Library of Congress, and the Academy of American Poets, Phillips teaches at Washington University, St. Louis.

Of "All Art . . . ," Phillips writes: "The poem began with a landscape photograph (taken by my partner, Doug Macomber) that had begun to warp inside its frame. From there, the idea of containment and a restiveness with being contained led me to the areas that have always engaged me: the body as something we govern and are governed by, the degree to which we can believably be said to be contained within some larger design (of nature, of whatever divinity might be), and the lengths to which (necessarily?) we abandon ourselves up to possible danger in the names, variously, of pleasure, hunger, devotion, art. The line in Robert Hayden's poem 'The Tattooed Man' ('All art is pain / suffered and outlived') was my source for the title."

ROBERT PINSKY was born in Long Branch, New Jersey, on October 20, 1940. He is serving a third term as Poet Laureate of the United States. In April 2000, his most recent book of poems, *Jersey Rain,* was published by Farrar, Straus and Giroux. He is coeditor of *Americans' Favorite Poems,* an anthology of poems introduced by readers who selected them, published by Norton in 1999.

Pinsky writes: "'Samurai Song' was inspired by a poem I heard read at one of the many Favorite Poem Project readings I have attended. The project, as well as the anthology *Americans' Favorite Poems* and the Web site at www.favoritepoem.org, has involved many readings in communities around the country. In Salina, Kansas, the readers, as I remember, included the mayor, some schoolchildren and other citizens including a welder who read a fourteenth-century Japanese poem based on the formula 'When I . . . then I . . .'

"In the plane on the way back to Boston I kept thinking about the formula, and it evoked familiar, tangled memories of my mother's head injury, her persistent inner-ear problems, the years of disarray that required each member of the family to devise a kind of code for survival. I thought about how those years were my version of universal trials: loneliness and deprivation that in different ways and degrees are part of every life. I had always found this material difficult to write about without self-pity in one direction, or a kind of existential grandiloquence in the other. The Japanese formula, stylizing both directions, seemed to give me a way out of the clichés of personal narrative in poetry. So I stole the formula, and wrote the poem on my flight home."

DONALD PLATT was born in Coral Gables, Florida, in 1957. His first book, *Fresh Peaches, Fireworks, & Guns,* was published by Purdue University Press in 1994 as the winner of the Verna Emery Poetry Prize. A letterpress chapbook, entitled *Leap Second at the Turn of the Millennium,* appeared in spring 2000 from the Center for Book Arts in New York City. A recipient of a fellowship from the National Endowment for the Arts, of the Paumanok Poetry Prize, and of *The Nation* / the "Discovery" Prize, he teaches at the State University of West Georgia and lives in Carrollton with his wife and two daughters.

Platt writes: "The first two-and-a-half tercets of 'History & Bikinis' lay around for five years in a notebook while I alternately forgot about them or fruitlessly tried to imagine the poem toward which they might lead. I think they must have been generated by my Uncle Martin's impending death, which my mother announced to me in a memorable card on my thirty-fifth birthday. She wrote, 'Uncle Mart has terminal cancer & and will not be able to visit. . . .'

"In the summer of 1997, I decided that it was time to do something with the image of my uncle gently rocking chickens to sleep before slaughtering them. I had been reading Taylor Branch's *Parting the Waters,* a history of Martin Luther King and the Civil Rights movement; I had also been dabbling in Heraclitus and Yeats and more assiduously reading 'Today in History,' a trivia column in our local newspaper. Such desultory reading and my own distorted memories led to 'History & Bikinis.' The first draft was finished quickly. I started writing at about midnight and was finished by 7:00 A.M.—in time to make breakfast for my two daughters. It took nine subsequent drafts, and some editorial suggestions by fellow poets, to arrive at this version of the poem."

STANLEY PLUMLY was born in 1939 in Barnesville, Ohio, a small Quaker community in Belmont County, near the Ohio River. He describes it as "a community that my family, on my father's side, helped to found at the turn of the eighteenth century and in which all my American fathers before me were born." "Kunitz Tending Roses" appears in *Now That My Father Lies Down Beside Me: New & Selected Poems, 1970–2000* (Ecco / HarperCollins, 2000).

Of "Kunitz Tending Roses," Plumly writes: "In the late seventies, when I lived in Manhattan, I used to visit Stanley Kunitz once in a while at his Greenwich Village apartment—a lovely brownstone, as I recall. It was usually a Sunday evening, spring or fall. I'd known and loved his poems for a long time—he was one of the first poets I read extensively, and the first, I think, whose passion for poetry was clear to me. I remember seeing him, however, before I met him, on television, oddly enough, in 1963, when he and Robert Lowell were being interviewed on the occasion of Theodore Roethke's death (Uncle Stanley was Roethke's nickname for him). It was one of those live Sunday morning shows on CBS that used to pay attention to the arts.

"Kunitz was born in 1905, Roethke in 1908, a fact that says a great deal about Kunitz's staying power. Thus when I first met him in the seventies he was already a senior and influential figure. And he had a rose garden—the Manhattan site a smaller, more intimate version of the now-famous Provincetown garden. He loved his roses the way he loved poetry, with passion. On any given Sunday, that's where we'd usually end up, behind his brownstone, with a glass of wine, talking roses. Now, more than twenty years later, he's still in his garden."

LAWRENCE RAAB was born in Pittsfield, Massachusetts, in 1946. He is the author of five collections of poetry, including *What We Don't Know about Each Other* (Penguin, 1993), which was a winner of the National Poetry Series and a finalist for the National Book Award. His most recent book is *The Probable World* (Penguin, 2000). He lives in Williamstown, Massachusetts, where he teaches literature and writing at Williams College.

Of "Permanence," Raab writes: "I always tell my students that they must feel free to change the facts of their experience if the truth of the poem demands it. But I have to admit that everything remembered in this poem actually happened. Except for our chemistry experiment, which went awry not in Michael's house but in mine. Somehow the syntax of the sentence required that unimportant adjustment. But each time I read the poem I'm reminded of this, as if my awareness of how the past is altered—and how much more I must have changed without knowing it—has become part of the poem's secret meaning, available only to me. Or to Michael. Whom I imagine writing to me some day to ask, 'But how can I trust anything you've said when you got something so simple wrong?'"

THOMAS RABBITT was born in Boston, Massachusetts, in 1943, and educated at the Boston Latin School and Harvard College. He taught at the University of Alabama from 1972 until 1998. His first book, *Exile,* won the 1974 "Pitt Prize" (the United States Award of the International Poetry Forum). His eighth collection, *Enemies of the State,* was published by Black Belt Press in January 2000. In 1997 Rabbitt was awarded literature fellowships from the Alabama Arts Council and the National Endowment for the Arts. He lives on a farm in the west of Ireland.

Of "The Beach at Falmouth Heights, Summer, 1952," Rabbitt writes: "Among those twentieth-century poems I find most affecting are Randall Jarrell's monologues spoken by female personae. No person moves me more than the woman of 'Seele im Raum.' My poem is an imitation and an homage.

"Every summer from 1956 to 1964, when I was a teenager, I worked on Falmouth Heights, in the kitchen of the Oak Crest Inn, a sprawling, dilapidated palace of sticks where my grandfather was the chef and my grandmother the laundress. The inn was put to the torch a decade ago. The poem takes place a few years before I arrived on the scene, during the Korean police action, the first war fully to occupy my consciousness, the first war the good guys could not claim they had won. When I was eight, a lady in my neighborhood in Boston asked me to pray for her son who was one of the troops left behind in the Hungnam evacuation. She had to hope he had been taken prisoner. Later, when the names of the released POWs were read on the radio, I listened for his name, but never heard it.

"Finally, although it is polite to say that a first-person speaker is not the poet but the poet's invention, the woman who speaks this poem is me, trying very hard to do what Jarrell did so brilliantly, breathing a true life into words."

MARY JO SALTER was born in Grand Rapids, Michigan, in 1954, and grew up mostly in Baltimore. A graduate of Harvard University and of Cambridge, she is Emily Dickinson Lecturer in the Humanities at Mount Holyoke College, where she has taught since 1984. She has also worked as a staff editor at *The Atlantic Monthly,* as poetry editor of *The New Republic,* and most recently, as coeditor of *The Norton Anthology of Poetry, 4th edition* (Norton, 1996). Her first collection of poems, *Henry Purcell in Japan* (Knopf, 1985), was followed by *Unfinished Painting* (Knopf, 1989), which won the Lamont Prize; *Sunday Skaters* (Knopf, 1994); and *A Kiss in Space* (Knopf, 1999). She has also published a children's book, *The Moon Comes Home* (Knopf, 1999). An essayist and reviewer, she is currently a columnist for an online magazine, *The Read,* at www.oxygen.com. She lives with her husband, the writer Brad Leithauser, and their two children in Amherst, Massachusetts.

Of "Au Pair," Salter writes: "Having spent many years of my life as a foreigner—in furnished temporary apartments from Kyoto to Reykjavík to Paris—I set myself the task of imagining what it must be like to be living in America for the first time. My family employed two French au pairs in Massachusetts over a span of a year, and these two young women—the first sullen and almost criminal, the second bouncy and warmhearted—fascinated me by volunteering first impressions of America that were eerily similar. I added a few invented touches and fused the two characters into one, unfairly. The poem was a liberation to write, technically speaking; though it rhymes, the rhyme scheme changes every stanza, and the meter is deliberately clunky. I aimed, too, at a small and mundane vocabulary—for veracity's sake."

REBECCA SEIFERLE was born in Denver, Colorado, in 1951, but grew up all over the country. The title poem of her second collection, *The Music We Dance To* (Sheep Meadow Press, 1999), won the Cecil Hemley Award from the Poetry Society of America (judge, Mark Jarman). Her first collection, *The Ripped-Out Seam* (Sheep Meadow Press, 1993) won the Bogin Award from the Poetry Society of America and the Writers' Exchange Award. She has also published a translation of Cesar Vallejo's *Trilce* (Sheep Meadow Press, 1992). She has lived in New Mexico since 1970 and has worked as an assistant housekeeper, a member of the New Mexico artists-in-the-schools program, and a librarian and substitute teacher at Navajo Academy, a prep school for gifted Navajo students. She teaches at San Juan Community College and lives in Farmington, New Mexico, with her husband and three children.

Of "Welcome to Ithaca," Seiferle writes: "I have always been troubled by the slaughter of the servant women in *The Odyssey*. In all the volumes that have been written in response to *The Odyssey*, I've never read a sentence that faced that appalling scene directly; it's been relegated to anecdote, forever interpreted as if from Odysseus's view. Elizabeth Bishop said a poem is a 'hundred things happening at once,' but I will mention just a few of the intersections that impelled this poem into being. First, the underlying experience. Having been in over twenty different schools all over the country by the time I graduated from high school was enough to teach me every connotation of the word 'visitor,' and the years I spent working at a local motel as an assistant housekeeper were all that I needed to know of the world of 'servant women,' of the way in which those who are ordered about are held accountable. But all of this submerged material came into being upon the hook of language. I was rereading *The Iliad* for the classes that I was teaching, and was struck by how Homer uses metaphor to shift the burden of blood guilt, so that the berserk rages of the Achaeans are compared to the movements of lions or waves or wolves, and therefore granted the same degree of 'necessity' or 'naturalness.' In the *OED* 'metaphor' is described as originating in two words, meaning to shift the burden from one thing to another. At the same time, I happened to be reading other books on poetics which insisted that the 'genius of poetry' is the 'genius of metaphor,' and became troubled by the complicity of language, the degree to which the poet may be said to sanctify blood-letting. It was this fear of complicity that began the poem. It was clear to me that the slaughter of the servant women is like all the slaughters of our time. Like those in the concentration camps, the women are made to dispose of the dead who were their lovers, before being killed themselves. As men were lined up single-file by the SS to see how many could be killed with a single bullet, the servant women are killed by Telemachus en masse, noosed on one string. In every case, the one killed is first turned into an animal or thing, and it is the poet's metaphor that grants this power. There is the curious story of Penelope's dream that foreshadows the killing when she sees her geese slaughtered around the water trough, which suggests some depth of ambivalence in her, a depth of feeling that is usually overlooked. But all in all, the metaphor is the means by which the human is reduced to the animal, a possession that may be slaughtered at will. Originally I called the poem 'Penelope's Dream' but when the poet Eleanor Wilner hesitated at the title, I agreed that it made the event seem too much of

Penelope's imagining, and in the freewheeling conversation of the moment, Eleanor said, 'Oh well, call it something, welcome to Ithaca,' and the name stuck. The other revision came after I had an unplanned meeting with a former teacher and friend, a meeting that was somewhat chilled, and when I said that I regretted there was no time to find out how she was doing, she kept insisting that this was as it should be, for I was 'the visitor.' The repetition of this term, in the chill of the moment, made me go home and change 'guest' to 'visitor' and 'he' to 'she,' for the threat here is gender-specific, and dismissiveness is the cold side of the vaunted code of hospitality."

BRENDA SHAUGHNESSY was born in Okinawa, Japan, in 1970, and grew up in Thousand Oaks, California. She received her BA in literature and in women's studies at the University of California, Santa Cruz, and her M.F.A. at Columbia University. Her first book of poems, *Interior with Sudden Joy,* was published in 1999 by Farrar, Straus and Giroux. She lives in New York City.

Of "Postfeminism," Shaughnessy writes: "I use the term sarcastically, since I don't believe for a minute that feminism is 'over.' It continues to evolve as a diasporic, shape-shifting, and simultaneous series of interrogations of society but also of souls. A lifelong exploration of how naked to be, how defensive, and with whom. What battles to pick and what to wear. I wanted to write about how feminism can be both menacing and humorous, dangerous and fun! A fraught ontological playground where the floor is a quicksand of self-doubt and inherited bullshit and the glass ceiling is mirrored. This poem is about feminism as a mostly interior struggle, with the carnal body linking that interiority to its equally complicated public existence, knowing that neither public nor private spaces are what they claim to be. The battle is not between men and women, but between self and other, a blurry distinction indeed. The two kinds of people in the world are 'you and me,' that is, personally defined and slippery. Who is predator and who is prey, yours or mine, subject or object, cop or perp, oscillates between any two people up for the feminist challenge of flummoxing power with eros."

LAURIE SHECK was born in the Bronx, New York, in 1953. Her most recent book of poems is *The Willow Grove* (Knopf, 1996). She has been the recipient of a Guggenheim Fellowship, two National Endowment for the Arts fellowships, and an Ingram Merrill Award. She currently teaches at Princeton University, and lives in Princeton with her husband and daughter.

Of "from *Black Series,*" Sheck writes: "This poem is part of a series that involves itself with images of rigidity (mannequins, Medusa's stare) and images of what might seem like the flip side of rigidity—pliancy, doubt, receptivity, dissolution. I think of the 'Black' in the title as a kind of psychological landscape, pointing toward feelings and sensations / ideas that are primal and not directly autobiographical.

"Through pacing, through hesitations and repetitions (among other things), Samuel Beckett, in his genius, made absence, silence, and unknowing feel eerily precise. Almost like a place. This interested me. And when I saw the work of the installation artist Ann Hamilton, I was struck by how she could take a space and turn it into an evocative experience, at once luminous and solemn. Suddenly those spaces seemed to become about radiance and thresholds and desire. They felt contemporary and archaic, layered and suggestive, and awake to the complexities of revealing and concealing. The speaker of my poem senses that nothing is simply revealed without also carrying its own form of concealment. Clarity, though we may long for it, is also constantly in danger of being too reductive—a form of imposture or disguise. The speaker of this poem is interested in concealment and encryption, and so experiences nightfall in a particular way."

REGINALD SHEPHERD was born in 1963 in New York City and raised in the Bronx. A great enthusiast of student financial aid, he has degrees from Bennington College, Brown University, and the University of Iowa. His first book, *Some Are Drowning,* was published by the University of Pittsburgh Press in 1994 as winner of the 1993 Associated Writing Programs Award. The University of Pittsburgh Press also published his second book, *Angel, Interrupted,* in 1996 and his third, *Wrong,* in 1999. After six years in Chicago (which he still direly misses), he currently lives in Ithaca, New York, and is an assistant professor of English at Cornell University.

Shepherd writes: "'Semantics at Four P.M.' had its genesis in an afternoon (closer to three than four) when a (now former) colleague of whom I wasn't terribly fond greeted me (as was his somewhat irritating wont) with the words 'What's happening?' and it occurred to me that all sorts of things were happening in all sorts of places about which he probably didn't want to know. I listed a few (hypothetical) examples, and it turned out that indeed he didn't want to know about them. The poem embraces the proximity of banality and brutality (as a friend put it, the mundaneness of life while all this is going on and how little any of it matters): itself a banal observation, which demonstrates the danger of discussing banality: one almost inevitably falls victim to the imitative fallacy.

"The poem's most interesting characteristic for me is its winding, roundabout syntax, accommodating any number of seemingly random elements without necessarily specifying their relations to one another: a suitable analogue to the poem's topic, since in DeKalb, Chicago, or Ithaca (to name a few places relevant to me) hackeysack is as real as or more real than the torture of some (to us) nameless and faceless Central American peasant in whose demise we are ultimately (some obviously much more, and less ultimately, than others) implicated. It does make one feel good to feel bad about the straits of far distant others, doesn't it?"

RICHARD SIKEN was born in New York City in 1967, but his parents moved him to Arizona when he was two and a half, and he has pretty much been there ever since. He is the recipient of an Arizona Commission on the Arts grant and his poems have appeared in *Chelsea, Conjunctions, Indiana Review, Iowa Review, Jackleg, The James White Review,* and *Sonora Review.* He started waiting tables to put himself through school. Now he is through with school and still waiting tables at a twenty-four-hour restaurant.

Of "The Dislocated Room," Siken writes: "There was this one time, after work, after the bar rush, after I had fed the drunks all the fried eggs and pancakes they could handle and had scraped the plates and wiped the tables, in that quiet hour between punching out and the arrival of the man from Donut Palace with his pink cardboard boxes, I was sitting with my friend Dave, reading to him, out loud, a poem by Anne Carson called 'The Book of Isaiah' and I had just gotten to the part where Isaiah addresses the Nation, and Dave says 'Wow! That's amazing! That's why Anne Carson will always be a better poet than you.' Now Dave and I are friends, but that doesn't mean we don't get ugly, and I could tell he meant what he said, even though he didn't mean to say it, and he tried to take it back but I wouldn't let it drop and so, finally, he blurts out, 'Why can't you just say what you mean? Your poems start out okay, but then they go all Francis Bacon in the middle.'

"Okay, we all know that Anne Carson will always be a better poet than me, there is a long list of reasons why, and I understand this, I have even come to terms with it, but I am actually somewhat bothered by this Francis Bacon business. Basically, Francis was a painter who got famous for making fucked-up, blurry pictures which, I guess, is what I am trying to do also. And yet, Dear Reader, Dear Nation, like Isaiah, I am trying to reach you. From here, where I have hands. I am not trying to be difficult. There is something up ahead, in the distance, waiting for you like a room or a mood, and it is sloppy, and it is messy, and I have seen it and I am trying to describe it to you with a different kind of precision. Unfortunately, unlike Isaiah, I am bad with facts and I make stuff up and I continue to fail to find a middle distance. And it doesn't help that this poem is the fifth in a series of nine, so that things that should be concrete and understandable, like the bullet and the dog, set up so well in previous poems, appear so suddenly and weirdly. Dave would have you believe that all of this just goes to show that I am an unreasonable man, and perhaps he's right, but you shouldn't ask your car for toast, you shouldn't ask your toaster to take you to the record store. A cornfield will still never give you snowpeas."

CATHY SONG was born in Honolulu, Hawai'i, in 1955. She holds degrees from Wellesley College and Boston University. In 1982 her first book, *Picture Bride,* won the Yale Series of Younger Poets Award and was nominated for the National Book Critics Circle Award. In 1988 Norton brought out *Frameless Windows, Squares of Light. School Figures,* her third collection of poetry, was published in 1994 in the Pitt Poetry Series of the University of Pittsburgh Press. Her poetry has been anthologized in *The Norton Anthology of Modern Poetry* and *The Norton Anthology of American Literature.* Now appearing on the buses in Atlanta as well as in subway cars throughout New York City, her poetry is part of the Poetry in Motion program. She is the recipient of a number of awards including the Frederick Bock Prize for poetry, the Shelley Memorial Award from the Poetry Society of America, the Hawaii Award for Literature, and a creative writing fellowship from the National Endowment for the Arts. She lives in Honolulu with her husband and three children.

Song writes: "'Mother of Us All' is one of those poems that arise from somewhere deeply rooted to the surface whole and intact. At such times all you can do to stop the trembling is bow your head in gratitude."

GARY SOTO was born in Fresno, California, in 1952. He is the author of nine poetry collections for adults, most notably *New and Selected Poems,* a 1995 finalist for both the *Los Angeles Times* Book Award and the National Book Award. *Living up the Street,* a volume of his recollections, received the Before Columbus Foundation's American Book Award. He has guest-edited an issue of *Ploughshares.* In 1999 he was honored with the Human and Civil Rights Award from the American Education Association, the Literature Award from Hispanic Heritage Foundation, and the PEN Center West Book Award for his young-adult short story collection *Petty Crimes.* For the Los Angeles Opera, he wrote the libretto to the opera "Nerdlandia." Altogether, his books for adults and young people have sold 1.3 million copies. He is a member of the Royal Chicano Navy, and is a professor of creative writing at the University of California at Riverside. He lives in Berkeley, California.

Of "Chit-Chat with the Junior League Women," Soto writes: "What kind of chitchat makes a middle-aged man recall his youth? There's none better than with the Junior League women. I arrived at a designer home in a Honda with roll-up windows and enough hair on my ears to knit into a coat. I was chosen to judge, I believe, fifth-grade stories from a local school, and sample some exotic finger food, plus swirl wine in the early afternoon. I did my duty; I judged the kids' writing and then leaned back with a fellow writer to look not upon the San Francisco Bay or the stand of swaying eucalyptus trees in the yard or the art work on the wall, but slyly at these women. We were nothing like their husbands, who were in the slaughterhouses of hi-tech businesses. No, we were both unemployed writers and our vista was the undergarments of mysterious women who were plying us with food and drink but nothing more. I made my chitchat, then drove home through the leafy hills, slept off my afternoon buzz, and woke to my wife in overalls and a hardy meal of homemade stew. A far better fare."

GABRIEL SPERA was born in 1966 in Staten Island, New York, raised in Scotch Plains, New Jersey, and educated at Cornell University. He lives in Los Angeles, where he edits a technical trade publication.

Spera writes: "'In a Field Outside the Town' is based on the corroborating accounts of the only three survivors of this incident. I believe that poetry has an obligation to history, both personal and public, and indeed succeeds best when it finds the intersection between the personal and the public. Poetry becomes part of our collective identity in ways that other historical or journalistic media cannot, and is perhaps better able to reflect and direct the conscience of a people. Of course,

I'm aware of how I am implicated in my decision to turn enormity into art; but it's the first job of a poet to ensure that history—personal and public—is neither erased nor rewritten.

"On a stylistic note, my use of indefinite articles and plain diction is meant to convey a sense of ordinariness, a sense that such atrocities can (and do) occur anywhere. My loosely rhymed quatrains have their roots in the 'In Memoriam' stanza of Tennyson."

A. E. STALLINGS was born in Champaign, Illinois, in 1968. She studied classics at the University of Georgia and Oxford University. Her first poetry collection, *Archaic Smile,* was chosen by Dana Gioia for the Richard Wilbur Award, and appeared from the University of Evansville Press (1999). Her poetry has been awarded the Eunice Tietjens Prize from *Poetry* and the James Dickey Poetry Prize from *Five Points.* She currently resides in Athens, Greece, with her husband, the journalist John Psaropoulos.

Of "Asphodel," Stallings writes: "As the epigraph suggests, the poem was triggered by a real moment and conversation, about which began to gather, in my memory, clusters of natural rhymes, and a shape. Our guide, a horsewoman involved in rescuing a native breed of Greek pony (the Skyros pony) from possible extinction, was broadly read and an expert on local flora and fauna. Nymphaion is in the lush north of Greece, near the Albanian border. This area in no way resembles the Greece of postcards, the Peloponnese and the islands, with their familiar dust-silver olive groves, old women in black, and patient donkeys. The north is green, mountainous, and wild, still home to bears, eagles, wild boars, and wolves, the animals of Homeric similes.

"Some years back, in Atlanta, I was in a Greek reading group that was working through the Homeric Hymn to Demeter. In the opening scene, where Persephone and other nymphs are gathering flowers in a meadow, a number of flowers are named: the orchid, hyacinth, narcissus, iris, crocus, and others (this may not be exact, being from memory). And I made a comment at the time that perhaps this was to symbolize a golden age before seasons, when all flowers bloomed simultaneously; because I could not imagine them all in bloom together. At least in my garden, crocuses came up before narcissuses, and so on. But in these alpine meadows in the north of Greece I saw all these things blooming together, wild. I was quite startled. But this goes to show that there is always a danger in doubting the literal truth of ancient poetry."

SUSAN STEWART was born in York, Pennsylvania, in 1952, and is Regan Professor of English at the University of Pennsylvania, where she teaches poetry and aesthetics. She is the author of three books of poetry, most recently *The Forest* (University of Chicago Press, 1995), three books of prose criticism, and numerous essays on contemporary art. In 1997 she was named a MacArthur Fellow.

Stewart writes: "'Wings' is the *W* of an alphabet of georgics and their shadows, which will be my next book of poems. The georgics are poems of instruction: some are paraphrases of Virgil and others are meditations on everyday life; they are spoken by a member of one generation to a member of another. A conversation I had with my oldest son, Jacob Stewart-Halevy, is the source for 'Wings.' The final lines are taken from one of Hermione's speeches in Euripides' *Andromache,* a play I am currently translating for Oxford University Press with the Hellenist Wesley Smith. These lines were rejected in our final draft of the play, but they seemed to belong here with their sense of incremental departure."

ADRIENNE SU was born in Atlanta in 1967. She is the author of the poetry collection *Middle Kingdom* (Alice James Books, 1997). She has received fellowships from Dartmouth College and the Fine Arts Work Center in Provincetown, Massachusetts. Her poems can be found in *The Bread Loaf Anthology of New American Poets* and *American Poetry: The Next Generation.* Su, who works as a freelance writer, also writes essays about food and cooking, which have appeared in *Prairie Schooner, Saveur,* and *The NuyorAsian Anthology.*

Su writes: "When I'm working on a poem, I try to establish a formal pattern, sometimes using rhyme, sometimes relying only on structural symmetry, which can mean as little as using stanzas with the same number of lines. In 'The English Canon,' I deliberately ended the first four stanzas with '-ing,' which is a kind of cheater's rhyme, and the last two with the imperfect rhyme of 'combat' and 'scratch.' I threw in 'protest' and 'trust' near the end, for fun. Between the cheating, the imperfection, and the distance between rhymes, I hope that the poem reads as free verse, yet looks formal because of the tercets. The combination of the free and constrained, of modern and traditional, seemed suited to the subject, writing to and from the canon."

PAMELA SUTTON was born in 1960 in Ypsilanti, Michigan, and currently works as a development editor for Lippincott Williams & Wilkins.

She has taught poetry at the University of Pennsylvania and, in 1995, was a teaching fellow at Boston University, where she received an M.A. in creative writing, studying with Robert Pinsky, Derek Walcott, and Alberto de Lacerda. She also received an MS in journalism from Northwestern University and a B.A. in English literature from Wheaton College. From 1989 to 1993 she worked as associate editor for the *American Poetry Review*. In 1999 she received a Pennsylvania Council on the Arts award in literature and in 1998 was a finalist for a Pew Fellowship in poetry. She has two book-length manuscripts of poetry and one novella—all looking for publishers. She has one child, Emily Brooke, who is three years old.

Of "There Is a Lake of Ice on the Moon," Sutton writes: "Sometimes closure is neither possible nor desirable, and I think this is a poem against the current trend in American thinking that we must always be 'getting on with our lives'—that after great pain we must seek closure. Rather, 'After great pain, a formal feeling comes—' (Emily Dickinson). And that is the place from which I wrote this poem—Emily Dickinson's 'Disc of snow' and Robert Frost's 'Desert Places.' Like Robert Frost, I spent some time in my twenties as an amateur astronomer—dragging a six-foot-tall Celestron telescope out to the lawn each night to examine the stars, which, to my surprise, were moving and breathing and vibrant, like the inverse of an earthly forest. Then, hearing one day on the news that a lake of ice had been found on the moon, I realized this was the perfect metaphor for my reluctance to seek conclusions in relationships, that there was a place in my interior landscape that would not allow closure—a place of stasis where time and emotion remain frozen. Long after I wrote the poem, I realized I must have been thinking specifically and unconsciously about Frost's poem 'Desert Places': 'They cannot scare me with their empty spaces / Between stars—on stars where no human race is. / I have it in me so much nearer home / To scare myself with my own desert places.' I wanted to write an addendum to that poem—I wanted to continue the story."

DOROTHEA TANNING was born in Galesburg, Illinois, in 1910. Most of her life has been devoted to painting and sculpture. Her works are in such major museum collections as the Centre Pompidou and the Musée de la Ville de Paris, both in Paris; the Tate Gallery, London; the Menil Collection, Houston; the Philadelphia Museum of Art; the Museum of Modern Art and the Whitney Museum, both in New York. Her forays into theater design (with Balanchine), architecture (a house in the south of France), writing (a memoir, essays, and poetry), and a thirty-four-year marriage have filled out a long and productive life on two continents. After twenty-eight years in France she returned in 1979 to New York, where the writing of poems gradually became, and continues to be, her best-loved activity. Daring at last to submit her poems to other eyes, she was blissfully gratified by seeing one of them, "No Palms," published in *The Yale Review.*

About "No Palms" she tells of driving at night through the California desert on the way to Los Angeles: "Looming in the headlights, a blue-and-white town marker, 'No Palms. Pop. 3,' preceded a filling station (faint light), a shack (no light), and, in the mind, an unforgettable mixture of reverie and desert dearth. The reverie and dearth, along with the phantom title, are what sparked the poem. From there it was a matter of conflict and image parading as metaphor, of a rhyme scheme to delight me, and a celebratory ending."

NATASHA TRETHEWEY was born in Gulfport, Mississippi, in 1966. She has received a fellowship from the National Endowment for the Arts and a Grolier Poetry Prize. Her poems have appeared or are forthcoming in *The American Poetry Review, Gettysburg Review, New England Review, Shenandoah,* and *The Southern Review. Domestic Work,* her first collection of poems, was chosen by Rita Dove for the 1999 Cave Canem Poetry Prize and will be published in fall 2000 by Graywolf Press. She is an assistant professor of English at Auburn University.

About "Limen," Trethewey writes: "I had been trying to write a poem about forgetting my mother's face for a long time in the years after her death. One day, sitting at my desk unable to write anything, I forced myself to attempt a sestina—something I'd never done. Because of the particular demands of the sestina, I soon found myself saying things that startled me. The repetition of certain words pushed me through a doorway into the emotional and psychological realm I was discovering through the poem. I finished it quickly, read it, then put it aside and took out another sheet of paper. Then, the work I had done with that first attempt, the forced sestina, enabled me to write 'Limen,' the poem I had been trying to write all along.

"One other thing: when I sent the poem to C. Dale Young, the poetry editor at *New England Review,* he suggested that I change my original title, 'Industry.' I had used that title, of course, to suggest not only the work of the woodpecker, but the work of memory as well. C. Dale was right; that title was indeed pedestrian. So I spent days rethinking it, asking my friends what they thought, and flipping through my dictionary until it hit me: *liminal*. Looking that word up I found *limen*—a threshold—the very place I had been as I sat at my desk listening to the insistent knocking of that woodpecker just outside my window."

QUINCY TROUPE is the author of twelve books, six of which are volumes of poetry: *Embryo* (Barlenmir House, 1972), *Snake-Back Solos* (Reed & Cannon, 1979) (winner of the 1980 American Book Award for Poetry), *Skulls Along the River* (I. Reed Books, 1984), *Weather Reports: New and Selected Poems* (Harlem River Press, 1991, rpt. 1996), and *Avalanche* (Coffee House Press, 1996). His sixth volume of poetry, *Choruses,* was published in November 1999 by Coffee House Press. He is the coauthor (with Miles Davis) of *Miles: The Autobiography* (winner of the 1990 American Book Award for nonfiction), and editor of *James Baldwin: The Legacy.* Both were published in 1989 by Simon and Schuster. Troupe is the recipient of a Peabody Award for *The Miles Davis Radio Project,* which he wrote and coproduced. In March 2000, the University of California Press published his critical memoir, *Miles and Me: A Memoir of Miles Davis,* and in fall 2000, Jump at the Sun, a division of Hyperion/Disney Books, will publish his "Poem for Magic" (for former basketball star Earvin "Magic" Johnson) as a book-length children's book with illustrations. He is finishing a novel, *The Footman Chronicles,* and is writing a memoir of his own life entitled *The Accordion Years: 1965 to 1998.* Troupe is the editorial director for *Code,* a monthly style magazine for "men of color." He is professor of Creative Writing and American and Caribbean Literature at the University of California, San Diego, and lives in La Jolla, California, with his wife, Margaret, and his son, Porter.

Troupe writes: "'Song' was the last poem written for my most recent book of poems *Choruses.* It was written as a response to another poem in this volume, 'Words That Build Bridges Toward a New Tongue.'

"Using colloquial speech, 'Words That Build Bridges Toward a New Tongue' is a free-flowing exercise in building a poetic text around a series of sounds, words, wordplays, cadences, rhymes, and rhythms fused into varied musical vocabularies like jazz, rock 'n' roll, blues, rap, rhythm 'n' blues. It is a kind of high-wire acrobatics of riffs, chants, snatches of popular songs, improvisation, and collage.

"In contrast, I felt that 'Song' should be a poem written in traditional form. But which one? Because many of the poems in the collection attempt to sing the language, I chose to write 'Song' as a villanelle, a songlike form constructed off two refrain lines used four times throughout a nineteen-line poem. Since *Choruses,* the title of the book and the title poem (dedicated to Allen Ginsberg), suggests song, and since for the first section, I had written a couple of sestinas, a villanelle, a few haikus strung together, and an extended blues, my idea was for both poems to serve as subtle anchors of a thematic arc that would guide the reader through my attempt to move from traditional poetic forms to improvisation.

"Moreover, by using the phrase words that build bridges toward a new tongue as both the first line of the book and as one of the refrain lines in 'Song,' I felt this would give the book the thematic arc that I desired and would also begin the book in the traditional way that I spoke of earlier. Then I could move the rest of the poems—gradually—toward a state of high improvisation, thus closing the book.

"Once I chose that first line of the poem, the mystery, magic, and music of poetic language took over, and I rode it like a musician rides a melody, or a surfer rides a wave. It was a wonderful experience."

REETIKA VAZIRANI was born in Punjab, India, in 1962, and moved to Maryland seven years later. She attended Wellesley College and the University of Virginia. *White Elephants* (Beacon, 1996) was selected by Marilyn Hacker for a Barnard New Women Poets Prize. She has received a Thomas J. Watson Fellowship, a "Discovery"/*The Nation* Award, and a fellowship from the Virginia Commission for the Arts. Poems from a new manuscript appear in *Callaloo, Prairie Schooner, AGNI,* and the *Bread Loaf Anthology of New American Poets,* edited by Michael Collier. A contributing editor of *Shenandoah,* she lives in Virginia and is the Banister Writer-in-Residence at Sweet Briar College.

Of "Rahim Multani," Vazirani writes: "Infidelity and transferred loyalties carry a double meaning for me as an immigrant. I was told, by what could be an unreliable source, that my mother's mother had an affair with a language tutor in pre-Independence India. My grandfather divorced her in 1944. Because of the upheaval, my mother was sent away to boarding school, and not too long afterwards my grandfather came to America with another wife. All kinds of ruptures, sexual and political. None of this gets discussed in my family. I am, it seems, always constructing a kind of family for myself. In 'Rahim Multani,' Maya seems divided and loyal. She's not at any rate going to tell the reader what actually happened, if anything did. Opposites flirt with each other. Prose and verse, too. It's a collage. I like the margins where the energy of images continues to buzz. Also, Richard Howard's *Untitled Subjects* has had much to do with how I imagined this poem as my family's dramas—his book remains astonishing to me, and I wanted to thank him."

PAUL VIOLI was born in New York in 1944 and grew up in Greenlawn, Long Island. After studying English literature and art history at Boston University, he traveled through Africa, Europe, and Asia, and then returned to New York, where he helped organize a reading series at the Museum of Modern Art for many years. His books include *The Curious Builder* and *Likewise* from Hanging Loose Press, *Splurge* and *Harmatan* from Sun Press, and *In Baltic Circles* from Kulchur Press. His latest books are *Fracas* (Hanging Loose Press, 1999) and a selection of his long poems, *Breakers* (Coffee House Press, 2000). The Foundation for Contemporary Performance Arts awarded him a grant in 1999. Violi teaches at New York University and Columbia.

Of "As I Was Telling David and Alexandra Kelley," Violi writes: "'Theories come and go, but anecdotes last forever'—Disraeli's observation, I think, but one that covers a concern or two of contemporary poetry.

"I first thought of the poem after relating the event it describes to Dave and Alex Kelley and noting the profound effect it had on them. I wrote it up as part of a book collaboration with Dale Devereaux Barker, *Selected Accidents, Pointless Anecdotes,* then reworked it into shorter lines to catch the tumbling rhythm I wanted. One problem was having too much to work with. I decided not to recount how the subject unwrapped a Christmas gift—a rototiller—and started it up on his plush living room carpet without knowing how to turn it off. And how, as he explained to the fire department, he attempted to remove a pine tree growing too close to his house by notching it around with a hatchet, soaking it in gasoline and—well, that was the idea, which I see under the umbrella of a greater idea that has certainly consoled me countless times, Augustine's 'I err, therefore I am.'"

DEREK WALCOTT was born in 1930 in St. Lucia, in the Windward Islands of the West Indies. He founded the Trinidad Theater Workshop, and his plays have been produced by the New York Shakespeare Festival, the Mark Taper Forum in Los Angeles, and the Negro Ensemble Company; *Dream on Monkey Mountain* won the Obie Award for distinguished foreign play of 1971. His twenty books of poetry include *Collected Poems: 1948–1984* (1986), *The Arkansas Testament* (1987),

Omeros (1990), *The Bounty* (1997), and *Tiepolo's Hound* (2000), all from Farrar, Straus and Giroux. *Tiepolo's Hound,* a book-length poem, contains twenty-five full-color reproductions of Walcott's own paintings. In 1981 he was named a MacArthur fellow. In 1992 he won the Nobel Prize for literature. During the academic year he teaches at Boston University. Otherwise he divides his time between his home in St. Lucia and New York City.

RICHARD WILBUR was born in New York City in 1921. He retired from academic life in 1986, having taught at Harvard, Wellesley, Wesleyan, and Smith. His latest book of poems, *Mayflies,* was published by Harcourt in April 2000. Story Line Press has recently reprinted (with additional material) his book of prose pieces called *Responses,* and two children's books are forthcoming from Harcourt. His translation of Molière's first five-act verse comedy, *The Bungler,* will initially be published by the Dramatists Play Service; two productions of the play are in the works. He and his wife live in Cummington, Massachusetts, and Key West, Florida.

Of "Fabrications," Wilbur writes: "Since 1965 or so, I've spent some part of every year in Key West, yet like Frost (and unlike Bishop and Stevens) I have been stuck with a New England imagination, and have been slow to see what the island might have to say in a poem. At long last I've found some words for that in a poem called 'Bone Key,' and it pleases me that the meandering thought of 'Fabrications' begins with a Key West perspective."

SUSAN WOOD was born in Commerce, Texas, on May 5, 1946. She is professor of English at Rice University in Houston, where she has taught for eighteen years. Prior to that she was a journalist; when she worked for the *Washington Post,* the best assignment she ever had was going on the road with Dolly Parton to the Wisconsin State Fair in Milwaukee. She has published two collections of poetry, *Bazaar* (Holt, Rinehart & Winston, 1981) and *Campo Santo* (Louisiana State University, 1991), and is completing a third, *Leafing. Campo Santo* won the Lamont prize of the Academy of American Poets and the Natalie Ornish prize of the Texas Institute of Letters. She has received fellowships from the National Endowment for the Arts and the Guggenheim Foundation. She has two adult children and a pug named Cosmo.

Wood writes: "'Analysis of the Rose as Sentimental Despair' is the title of a series of five paintings by Cy Twombley in the Menil Collection in Houston. The poem was commissioned as part of a program in memory of Dominique de Menil; along with other Houston poets, I was asked to write a poem relating to one of the works in the collection, but I had, in fact, already been thinking about this poem before I was asked to write it. The paintings are large abstractions in shades of pink and red, each containing a quote from one of three poets—Rumi, Rilke, and Leopardi—pertaining in some way to grief or loss, a subject all three poets knew well. I'd been reading a lot of Rilke and also a biography of Rilke and thinking about what seemed to me his love of sadness—it's possible to love one's grief too much, I think. And I'd been thinking about mourning—my friend, the poet Larry Levis, a man who had seemed often sad, had died in 1996. Of course, what I'd been really struggling with was my own sadness, my own despair, and trying to answer the question of what is enough, of how to live. What seemed truest to me, though, for Rilke as well as for Larry—and what Twombley knows in those wonderful paintings—is the courage it takes to know despair, to look at death closely, and still to desire to go on writing poems and living. Larry had struggled through a lot of difficulties in his life and had found that courage. It's what Rilke says at the end of the fourth of the *Duino Elegies:* 'That one can contain death . . . can hold it to one's heart gently, and not refuse to go on living, is inexpressible.'"

JOHN YAU was born in Lynn, Massachusetts, in 1950, shortly after his parents left Shanghai. He received a BA from Bard College and an MFA from Brooklyn College. By choice, he is a poet, fiction writer, art critic, curator, editor, publisher, and teacher. He has taught at Brown University, the University of California, Berkeley, and the Maryland Institute, College of Art. In the 1990s he lived in Berkeley and Berlin and spent time in Los Angeles. Manhattan, however, always pulls him back to its vertical island. He has published more than a dozen books of poetry: *Radiant Silhouette: New & Selected Work 1974–1988* (1989); *Edificio Sayonara* (1992) and *Forbidden Entries* (1996) are among recent collections published by Black Sparrow. He has also written two books of fiction, *Hawaiian Cowboys* (1995) and *My Symptoms* (1998), both from Black Sparrow, and at least eight books or monographs on contemporary artists, including *In the Realm of Appearances: The Art of Andy Warhol* (Ecco, 1993), *The United States of Jasper Johns* (Zoland, 1996), *Ed Moses Paintings and Drawings 1951–1996* (Museum of Contemporary Art, Los Angeles 1996) and *Dazzling Water, Dazzling Light: Recent Paintings of Pat Steir* (Hard Press, 2000). Between 1978 and 1995, his reviews and essays regularly appeared in such magazines as *Art in America, Artforum, ARTnews*, and *Arts*. In 1999 he edited *Fetish*, an anthology of fiction. Under the imprint Black Square Editions, he has published the work of various American and European authors. He has a book of essays on poetry and art forthcoming from the University of Michigan Press.

Yau writes: "'Borrowed Love Poems' is the title sequence of my next book of poems. The borrowings, which recur throughout, are from Osip Mandelstam and Robert Desnos. Their lines generated the individual poems in the sequence, but not the unfolding—that seems linked to a life lived in time. Whose life? Anyone who has been in love, I would like to think. One reason to write a sequence of lyric poems on the subject of love in the late 1990s is that it seemed to be something that couldn't or shouldn't be done. As my father was half English and half Chinese, born at a time when miscegenation laws were in effect in many parts of the world, doing something that shouldn't or couldn't be done was an act of necessity—like the word 'love.'"

DEAN YOUNG was born in Columbia, Pennsylvania, in 1955. He has received a fellowship from the Fine Arts Work Center in Provincetown, Massachusetts, a Stegner fellowship from Stanford University, and two fellowships from the National Endowment for the Arts. He has published four books of poems including *Strike Anywhere*, which won the Colorado Poetry Prize, and *First Course in Turbulence* (University of Pittsburgh Press, 1999). He is an associate professor at Loyola University and lives in Chicago and in Berkeley, California, with his wife, the fiction writer Cornelia Nixon, and cat, Minnow.

Young writes: "I made a collage with the same title while I was writing 'The Infirmament.' It shows, in part, a man (cut from the safety diagram in the seat pocket in front of you) sliding either out of or into a snarl of colored pencil and oil pastel. The poem started with the phrases that were flat and assertive, authoritative in a way that nearly masked their being conjectural. I followed that current for a while and then another sort of statement emerged, more observational but just as sure of itself. That in turn morphed to the resignation at the end of the poem, and I was happy with the shape the whole poem made, from certainty to a larger drenching of fact in emotion to a release into matters that have little concern for us. There are forces much more assertive than our own at work, and we flee only to come to another further beyond our control."

MAGAZINES WHERE THE POEMS
WERE FIRST PUBLISHED

American Letters & Commentary, ed. Anna Rabinowitz. 850 Park Avenue, Suite 5B, New York, NY 10021.

The American Poetry Review, eds. Stephen Berg, David Bonanno, and Arthur Vogelsang. 1721 Walnut Street, Philadelphia, PA 19103.

The Antioch Review, poetry ed. Judith Hall. P.O. Box 148, Yellow Springs, OH 45387.

The Atlantic Monthly, poetry ed. Peter Davison. 77 North Washington Street, Boston, MA 02114.

Barrow Street, eds. Andrea Carter Brown, Peter Covino, Ron Drummond, Lois Hirshkowitz, and Melissa Hotchkiss. P.O. Box 2017, Old Chelsea Station, New York, NY 10113-2017.

Beloit Poetry Journal, ed. Marion K. Stocking. RFD 2, Box 154, Ellsworth, ME 04605.

Black Warrior Review, poetry ed. Matt Doherty. P.O. Box 862936, Tuscaloosa, AL 35486-0027.

Boston Book Review, ed. Theoharis Constantine Theoharis. 30 Brattle Street, 4th Floor, Cambridge, MA 02138.

Boston Review, poetry eds. Mary Jo Bang and Timothy Donnelly. E53-407, MIT, 30 Wadsworth Street, Cambridge, MA 02139-4307.

Boulevard, ed. Richard Burgin. 4579 Laclede Avenue, #332, St. Louis, MO 63108-2103.

Callaloo, ed. Charles H. Rowell. Department of English, 322 Bryan Hall, University of Virginia, Charlottesville, VA 22903.

Chelsea, ed. Richard Foerster. P.O. Box 773, Cooper Station, New York, NY 10276-0773.

Crab Orchard Review, poetry ed. Allison Joseph. English Department, Faner Hall, Southern Illinois University at Carbondale, Carbondale, IL 62901-4503.

Denver Quarterly, poetry ed. Bin Ramke. Department of English, University of Denver, Denver, CO 80208.

Five Points, eds. David Bottoms and Pam Durban. Georgia State University, University Plaza, Atlanta, GA 30303-3083.

The Georgia Review, ed. Stanley W. Lindberg. University of Georgia, Athens, GA 30602.

The Germ, eds. Andrew Maxwell and Macgregor Card. P.O. Box 8501, Santa Cruz, CA 95061.

The Gettysburg Review, ed. Peter Stitt. Gettysburg College, Gettysburg, PA 17325.

Harvard Review, poetry ed. David Rivard. Poetry Room, Harvard College Library, Cambridge, MA 02138.

Indiana Review, ed. Brian Leung. Indiana University, 465 Ballantine Hall, Bloomington, IN 47405.

Meridian, ed. Ted Genoways. Department of English, University of Virginia, Charlottesville, VA 22903.

New American Writing, eds. Paul Hoover and Maxine Chernoff. 369 Molino Avenue, Mill Valley, CA 94941.

The New Criterion, poetry ed. Robert Richman. 850 Seventh Avenue, New York, NY 10019.

New England Review, poetry ed. C. Dale Young. Middlebury College, Middlebury, VT 05753.

New Letters, ed. James McKinley. University of Missouri–Kansas City, Kansas City, MO 64110.

The New Yorker, poetry ed. Alice Quinn. 20 West 43rd Street, New York, NY 10036.

The New Republic, poetry ed. Charles Wright. 1220 19th Street NW, Washington, DC 20036.

Parnassus, ed. Herbert Leibowitz, 205 West 89th Street (8F), New York, NY 10024.

Partisan Review, poetry ed. Rosanna Warren. Boston University, 236 Bay State Road, Boston, MA 02215.

Ploughshares, eds. Don Lee and David Daniel. Emerson College, 100 Beacon Street, Boston, MA 02116.

Poetry, ed. Joseph Parisi. 60 West Walnut Street, Chicago, IL 60610-3380.

Poetry Daily, eds. Rob Anderson, Diane Boller, and Don Selby. www.poems.com.

Quarterly West, poetry eds. Danielle Dubrasky and Melanie Figg. 200 South Central Campus Drive, Room 317, University of Utah, Salt Lake City, UT 84112.

Seneca Review, ed. Deborah Tall. Hobart and William Smith Colleges, Geneva, NY 14456-3397.

Shenandoah, ed. R. T. Smith. Troubadour Theater, 2nd Floor, Washington and Lee University, Lexington, VA 24450-0303.

The Southern Review, poetry eds. James Olney and Dave Smith. 43 Allen Hall, Louisiana State University, Baton Rouge, LA 70803.

The Threepenny Review, ed. Wendy Lesser. P.O. Box 9131, Berkeley, CA 94709.

Tin House, poetry ed. Amy Bartlett. P.O. Box 10500, Portland, OR 97296.

TriQuarterly, ed. Susan Hahn. 2020 Ridge Avenue, Evanston, IL 60208.

The Virginia Quarterly Review, poetry ed. Gregory Orr. P.O. Box 400223, 1 West Range, Charlottesville, VA 22904-4223.

The World, ed. Ed Friedman. The Poetry Project, St. Mark's Church-in-the-Bowery, 131 East 10th Street, New York, NY 10003.

Xconnect, ed. D. Edward Deifer. http://ccat.sas.upenn.edu/xconnect or P.O. Box 2317, Philadelphia, PA 19103.

The Yale Review, ed. J. D. McClatchy. P.O. Box 208243, New Haven, CT 06520-8243.

ACKNOWLEDGMENTS

The series editor thanks his assistant, Mark Bibbins, for his invaluable work on this book. Warm thanks go also to Glen Hartley and Lynn Chu of Writers' Representatives, and to Gillian Blake, Jay Schweitzer, Erich Hobbing, Giulia Melucci, Kim Hilario, and Rachel Sussman of Scribner.

Grateful acknowledgments is made of the publications from which the poems in this volume were chosen. Unless specifically noted otherwise, copyright to the poems is held by the individual poets.

Kim Addonizio: "Virgin Spring" appeared in *Barrow Street*. Reprinted by permission of the poet.

Pamela Alexander: "Semiotics" appeared in *Boston Book Review*. Reprinted by permission of the poet.

A. R. Ammons: "Shot Glass" appeared in *The New Yorker*, February 15, 1999. Reprinted by permission; copyright © 1999 by A. R. Ammons.

Julianna Baggott: "Mary Todd on Her Deathbed" appeared in *Quarterly West*. Reprinted by permission of the poet.

Erin Belieu: "Choose Your Garden" from *One Above & One Below*. Copyright © 2000 by Erin Belieu. Reprinted by permission of the poet and Copper Canyon Press. First appeared in *TriQuarterly*.

Richard Blanco: "Mango, Number 61" from *City of a Hundred Fires* by Richard Blanco. Copyright © 1998 by Richard Blanco. Reprinted by permission of the poet and the University of Pittsburgh Press. First appeared in *TriQuarterly*.

Janet Bowdan: "The Year" appeared in *Denver Quarterly*. Reprinted by permission of the poet.

Grace Butcher: "Crow Is Walking" appeared in *Poetry*, copyright © 1999 by Grace Butcher. Reprinted by permission of the poet and the Editor of *Poetry*.

Lucille Clifton: "Signs" appeared in *Callaloo*. Reprinted by permission of the poet.

THE BEST
AMERICAN POETRY
OF THE TWENTIETH
CENTURY

◊   ◊   ◊

THE BEST AMERICAN POETRY
OF THE TWENTIETH CENTURY

Now that Y2K hoopla has given way to dot.com hysteria, it has become possible to speak of the twentieth century as a whole and irresistible to compile and exchange lists of our favorite poems of the last one hundred years. Which works are indispensable? Which do we feel we cannot do without? Which stand the best chance of enduring? Which do we simply like the best? Which have come to mean the most to us?

We make this first tentative effort toward answering these questions in the full consciousness that succeeding generations will modify, change, even reverse many of our judgments. We know, too, that any method we might use is flawed in some way. Still, it is a task worth doing, and worth doing well, if only as a record of the taste of some of our leading poets as they survey the monuments of what Henry Luce called the American century.

How to proceed? It seemed logical to poll the current and previous guest editors of *The Best American Poetry*. Each was asked (or implored) to name his or her top fifteen American poems of the twentieth century. The editors were given maximum latitude in how they defined "best" and "American." We deemed both Auden (born in York, England, moved to New York) and Eliot (born in St. Louis, Missouri, moved to London) eligible for inclusion.

Adrienne Rich declined to participate. So, too, did Louise Glück, who consented to write a statement explaining her decision. Richard Howard gave the names of sixteen poets but opted to cite the titles not of individual poems but of "the books in which their preferred poems are to be found."

Like Howard, Donald Hall and Mark Strand simplified the task a little by limiting themselves to poems by deceased poets. Acknowledging that his own taste is constantly evolving (as is true for most of us), Strand elected to "remain loyal to [his] feelings," listing poems that may have lost favor with him recently but had long served him well. Jorie Graham disavowed "terms such as indispensable or essential": she was declaring her favorites, not universalizing her taste. Rita Dove titled her list "fifteen great American poems of the twentieth century."

Charles Simic did not shy from choosing two poems by the same poet; he was unique in this regard. Some of the editors couldn't resist listing a sixteenth choice, or an honorable mention of works that barely missed the cut. In a few cases the poets couldn't make up their minds between two worthy poems by the same poet.

Some editors kept in mind the exigencies of length that govern the making of an anthology; others, liberated by the notion that this anthology may exist only as the Platonic conception of itself, elected to go with the whole of Hart Crane's *The Bridge,* T. S. Eliot's *Four Quartets,* James Merrill's *The Changing Light at Sandover,* or Ezra Pound's *The Cantos* rather than, say, "The River" from *The Bridge,* "Little Gidding" from *Four Quartets,* "The Book of Ephraim" from *The Changing Light at Sandover,* or Pound's Canto One.

One might expect a natural bias in favor of poems from the first three quarters of the century. With greater distance comes greater certitude. It is all the more noteworthy therefore that you will find one of John Ashbery's nominees—Christopher Edgar's "Birthday"—in the book you hold in your hands, for Rita Dove chose it from the pool of poems appearing in 1999 for *The Best American Poetry 2000.*

The lists are presented in chronological order of the volume of *The Best American Poetry* that the poet edited. The titles within the lists are arranged in alphabetical order. The composite list consists of poets whose work was nominated by at least two editors. It is also arranged in alphabetical order.

While we hope these lists stimulate discussion, even controversy, our greater hope is to call attention to poems that have given us equal measures of delight and instruction.

—DAVID LEHMAN

John Ashbery, Guest Editor
The Best American Poetry 1988

◊   ◊   ◊

A. R. Ammons, "Easter Morning"
W. H. Auden, "Paysage Moralisé" ("Hearing of harvests rotting in the valleys")
Elizabeth Bishop, "Over 2000 Illustrations and a Complete Concordance"
Robert Creeley, "Kitchen"
Christopher Edgar, "Birthday"
Kenneth Koch, "The Circus" [from *Thank You*]
Ann Lauterbach, "Prom in Toledo Night"
Marianne Moore, "An Octopus"
Frank O'Hara, "Memorial Day 1950"
David Schubert, "Kind Valentine"
James Schuyler, "Money Musk"
Delmore Schwartz, "Far Rockaway"
Wallace Stevens, "Chocorua to Its Neighbor"
James Tate, "Distance from Loved Ones"
John Yau, "Predella"

RUNNERS-UP

T. S. Eliot, "The Waste Land"
Samuel Greenberg, "East River's Charm"
Laura Riding, "Auspice of Jewels"
Gertrude Stein, *Stanzas in Meditation*
John Wheelwright, "Train Ride"
William Carlos Williams, *Kora in Hell*

Donald Hall, Guest Editor
The Best American Poetry 1989

◊   ◊   ◊

John Berryman, 77 *Dream Songs*
Elizabeth Bishop, "One Art"
Hart Crane, "Voyages"
T. S. Eliot, "Little Gidding"
Robert Frost, "To Earthward"
Robert Lowell, "Sister Marie Therese"
Marianne Moore, "The Steeple-Jack"
Frank O'Hara, "The Day Lady Died"
Ezra Pound, "Homage to Sextus Propertius"
Kenneth Rexroth, "The Signature of All Things"
Edwin Arlington Robinson, "Eros Turannos"
Theodore Roethke, "The Rose"
Wallace Stevens, "The Idea of Order at Key West"
Richard Wilbur, "A Baroque Wall-Fountain in the Villa Sciarra"
William Carlos Williams, "Spring and All"

Jorie Graham, Guest Editor
The Best American Poetry 1990

◊   ◊   ◊

Terms such as "indispensable" or "essential" make me uncomfortable.
What follows is simply a list of my own favorites:

John Ashbery, "Self-Portrait in a Convex Mirror"
W. H. Auden, "In Praise of Limestone" (original version)
John Berryman, 77 *Dream Songs*
Elizabeth Bishop, "At the Fishhouses"
Hart Crane, "Voyages"
Robert Creeley, "Histoire de Florida"
Robert Duncan, "A Poem Beginning with a Line by Pindar"
T. S. Eliot, "The Waste Land"
Robert Frost, "Home Burial" or "West-Running Brook"
Robert Hayden, "Middle Passage"
James Merrill, *The Changing Light at Sandover*
Ezra Pound, *The Cantos*
Gertrude Stein, *Tender Buttons*
Wallace Stevens, "The Auroras of Autumn"
William Carlos Williams, "Spring and All" (whole sequence)

16: Anthony Hecht, "Rites and Ceremonies"

Note: I have privileged long poems, a legacy of American mod-
ernism. As a result, it seems to me that Elizabeth Bishop, for
example, would be more fairly represented by the whole of *A
Cold Spring* (1955) than by any individual poem therein. The
same is the case for Robert Frost's *North of Boston* (1914) and
West-Running Brook (1928). Had I additional slots I would have
included poems by Marianne Moore, A. R. Ammons, George
Oppen, and James Wright, among others.

Mark Strand, Guest Editor
The Best American Poetry 1991

◇ ◇ ◇

These are poems I may not love as much as I once did, but I remain loyal to my feelings:

W. H. Auden, "In Praise of Limestone"
John Berryman, 77 *Dream Songs*
Elizabeth Bishop, "At the Fishhouses"
Hart Crane, "Voyages"
T. S. Eliot, "The Waste Land"
Robert Frost, "After Apple-Picking"
Robert Lowell, "The Quaker Graveyard in Nantucket"
James Merrill, "Lost in Translation"
Howard Moss, "King Midas"
Frank O'Hara, "To the Film Industry in Crisis"
Theodore Roethke, "The Lost Son"
James Schuyler, "The Morning of the Poem"
Wallace Stevens, "The Comedian as the Letter C"
Robert Penn Warren, "Audubon"
William Carlos Williams, "The Crimson Cyclamen"

Note: I included only deceased poets. If there were a sixteenth, I'd choose Marianne Moore's "What Are Years?" or possibly the first version of her "The Steeple-Jack."

Charles Simic, Guest Editor
The Best American Poetry 1992

◊ ◊ ◊

John Ashbery, "Self-Portrait in a Convex Mirror"
Elizabeth Bishop, "Sestina"
Elizabeth Bishop, "The Armadillo"
Gwendolyn Brooks, "The Lovers of the Poor"
Hart Crane, "At Melville's Tomb"
Robert Creeley, "I Know a Man"
T. S. Eliot, *Four Quartets*
Robert Frost, "Stopping by Woods on a Snowy Evening"
Robert Frost, "Design"
Robert Hayden, "Witch Doctor"
Robert Lowell, "For the Union Dead"
Ezra Pound, "Homage to Sextus Propertius"
William Stafford, "Travelling through the Dark"
Wallace Stevens, "The Comedian as the Letter C"
William Carlos Williams, "Asphodel, That Greeny Flower"

Louise Glück, Guest Editor
The Best American Poetry 1993

The Best American Poetry, in a given year, is, as its title says, a culling of what seems to a particular editor the best of what the magazines offered. The interest of the volumes, as they accumulate, is partly discovery and partly comparison: the magazines vary, year to year, but so too do the definitions of what constitutes the exceptional. And seventy-five poems make up a sample generous enough to take some of the pressure from the uneasy adjective: I tried, as I read those magazines, to put "best" from my mind, to replace it with terms that suggested versions of the memorable.

But the culling of a century is not the culling of a year's uncollected work. It is a culling of greatness. And in the twentieth century, a great deal of greatness. It seems to me not only impossible to choose so few but also misleading, false, to extend a problematic terminology: there can't be, I think, the best of the great.

A great work of art is an absolute. In its presence, all experience seems to adhere to it, to be included in it; the world conforms to its terms as though there need be no other terms. We feel, as readers, something like electric satiation, and a sense of majestic order: *this* is what was lacking, this poem. Which is to say, we feel something of what Copernicus may have felt staring at the heavens.

But in fact the kind of absolute art makes is not like that, not like astronomical order: a great truth in whose inescapable presence all other theories are reduced to postulates. It is like the spectrum, each absolute allowing for others, as red allows for blue.

What remains is preference. And I cannot, I find, prefer merely fifteen.

A. R. Ammons, Guest Editor
The Best American Poetry 1994

◇　◇　◇

John Ashbery, "The Painter"
Hart Crane, "The Broken Tower"
e. e. cummings, "All in green went my love riding"
Richard Eberhart, "The Groundhog"
Robert Frost, "The Most of It"
Langston Hughes, "The Weary Blues"
Randall Jarrell, "The Death of the Ball Turret Gunner"
Robinson Jeffers, "Hurt Hawks"
Denise Levertov, "The Dead Butterfly"
Marianne Moore, "Poetry"
Ezra Pound, "Canto One" (from *The Cantos*)
John Crowe Ransom, "Bells for John Whiteside's Daughter"
Theodore Roethke, "Root Cellar"
Wallace Stevens, "The Bird with the Coppery, Keen Claws"
William Carlos Williams, "Poem" ["as the cat / climbed over / the
    top of // the jamcloset . . ."]

RUNNERS-UP

X. J. Kennedy, "Emily Dickinson in Southern California"
Josephine Miles, "Reason"
Howard Nemerov, "Brainstorm"

Richard Howard, Guest Editor
The Best American Poetry 1995

◊   ◊   ◊

Fifteen (favorite) American poets (none living) and the books in which their preferred poems are to be found:

Elizabeth Bishop, *Geography III*
Louise Bogan, *The Blue Estuaries*
Hart Crane, *The Bridge*
T. S. Eliot, *Four Quartets*
Robert Frost, *North of Boston*
Randall Jarrell, *The Lost World*
Robert Lowell, *Life Studies*
James Merrill, *Late Settings*
Marianne Moore, *Observations*
Ezra Pound, *Personae*
John Crowe Ransom, *Grace After Meals*
E. A. Robinson, *The Town Down the River*
Allen Tate, *The Swimmers & Other Poems*
Robert Penn Warren, *Or Else*
Elinor Wylie, *Black Armour*

16: Theodore Roethke, *The Waking*

Adrienne Rich, Guest Editor
The Best American Poetry 1996

◇ ◇ ◇

Adrienne Rich, the editor of *The Best American Poetry 1996,* declined to participate.

James Tate, Guest Editor
The Best American Poetry 1997

◊　◊　◊

A. R. Ammons, "Corsons Inlet"
John Ashbery, *Flow Chart*
Elizabeth Bishop, "The Moose"
Hart Crane, "The River" (from *The Bridge*)
Russell Edson, "The Neighborhood Dog"
Robert Frost, "Directive"
Richard Hugo, "Montesano Unvisited"
W. S. Merwin, "Departure's Girl-Friend"
Sylvia Plath, "The Bee Meeting"
Theodore Roethke, "Praise to the End!"
Charles Simic, "The Devils"
Wallace Stevens, "The Man on the Dump"
William Carlos Williams, "Asphodel, That Greeny Flower"
Charles Wright, "Two Stories"
James Wright, "A Blessing"

John Hollander, Guest Editor
The Best American Poetry 1998

◇　◇　◇

John Ashbery, "Soonest Mended"
W. H. Auden, "In Praise of Limestone"
John Berryman, "Homage to Mistress Bradstreet"
Elizabeth Bishop, "Roosters"
Hart Crane, "The Bridge"
T. S. Eliot, "Little Gidding"
Robert Frost, "Directive"
James Merrill, "The Book of Ephraim"
Marianne Moore, "What Are Years?"
Edwin Arlington Robinson, "Eros Turannos"
Wallace Stevens, "The Auroras of Autumn"
May Swenson, "Satanic Form"
Robert Penn Warren, "Red-Tail Hawk and Pyre of Youth"
Richard Wilbur, "The Mind-Reader"
William Carlos Williams, "the rose is obsolete" (from *Spring
    And All*)

Note: If *The Bridge* isn't allowed as a single poem, then "To
Brooklyn Bridge." If either of the transatlantic problematics,
Auden and Eliot, is not allowed, then substitute Allen Ginsberg,
"America," or Anthony Hecht, "The Venetian Vespers." This
was *very* hard to select.

Robert Bly, Guest Editor
The Best American Poetry 1999

◇ ◇ ◇

Hart Crane, "Voyages I-VI"
Robert Creeley, "Love Comes Quietly"
T. S. Eliot, "The Waste Land"
Robert Frost, "After Apple-Picking"
Galway Kinnell, "The Bear"
Etheridge Knight, "The Idea of Ancestry"
Thomas McGrath, "The Bread of This World; Praises III"
Marianne Moore, "In Distrust of Merits"
Kenneth Rexroth, "The Heart of Herakles"
Edwin Arlington Robinson, "Miniver Cheevy"
William Stafford, "A Ritual to Read to Each Other"
Wallace Stevens, "Sunday Morning"
Richard Wilbur, "Love Calls Us to the Things of This World"
William Carlos Williams, "Beautiful Thing" or "Asphodel, That
    Greeny Flower"
James Wright, "Lying in a Hammock at William Duffy's Farm in
    Pine Island, Minnesota"

Rita Dove, Guest Editor

The Best American Poetry 2000

◊ ◊ ◊

Elizabeth Bishop, "The Fish"
Gwendolyn Brooks, "We Real Cool"
Countee Cullen, "To John Keats, Poet. At Springtime"
T. S. Eliot, "The Love Song of J. Alfred Prufrock"
Robert Frost, "Stopping by Woods on a Snowy Evening"
Allen Ginsberg, "Howl"
Robert Hayden, "Middle Passage"
Langston Hughes, "Dream Boogie"
Randall Jarrell, "Next Day"
James Merrill, "The Book of Ephraim"
Sylvia Plath, "Daddy"
Adrienne Rich, "Diving into the Wreck"
Melvin Tolson, "Harlem Gallery, Book I: The Curator"
William Carlos Williams, "The Red Wheelbarrow"
James Wright, "Lying in a Hammock at William Duffy's Farm in
    Pine Island, Minnesota"

David Lehman, Series Editor

The Best American Poetry

◇　◇　◇

A. R. Ammons, "Still"
John Ashbery, "The Skaters"
W. H. Auden, "In Praise of Limestone"
Elizabeth Bishop, "Crusoe in England"
Hart Crane, *The Bridge*
T. S. Eliot, "The Waste Land"
Robert Frost, "Birches"
Kenneth Koch, "The Railway Stationery"
James Merrill, "The Book of Ephraim"
Marianne Moore, "Marriage"
Frank O'Hara, "Why I Am Not a Painter"
James Schuyler, "The Morning of the Poem"
Delmore Schwartz, "Coriolanus and His Mother"
Gertrude Stein, *Tender Buttons*
Wallace Stevens, "The Snow Man"

RUNNERS-UP

W. H. Auden, "Caliban to the Audience" and "The More Loving
    One"
John Berryman, 77 *Dream Songs*
Allen Ginsberg, "America"
Ezra Pound, "Hugh Selwyn Mauberly"
William Carlos Williams, "Spring and All"

Composite List:
The Best American Poets of
the Twentieth Century

◊ ◊ ◊

A. R. Ammons
W. H. Auden
John Ashbery
John Berryman
Elizabeth Bishop
Gwendolyn Brooks
Hart Crane
Robert Creeley
T. S. Eliot
Robert Frost
Robert Hayden
Langston Hughes
Randall Jarrell
Kenneth Koch
Robert Lowell
James Merrill

Marianne Moore
Frank O'Hara
Sylvia Plath
Ezra Pound
Kenneth Rexroth
Edwin Arlington Robinson
Theodore Roethke
James Schuyler
Delmore Schwartz
William Stafford
Gertrude Stein
Wallace Stevens
Robert Penn Warren
Richard Wilbur
William Carlos Williams
James Wright

GAYLORD R